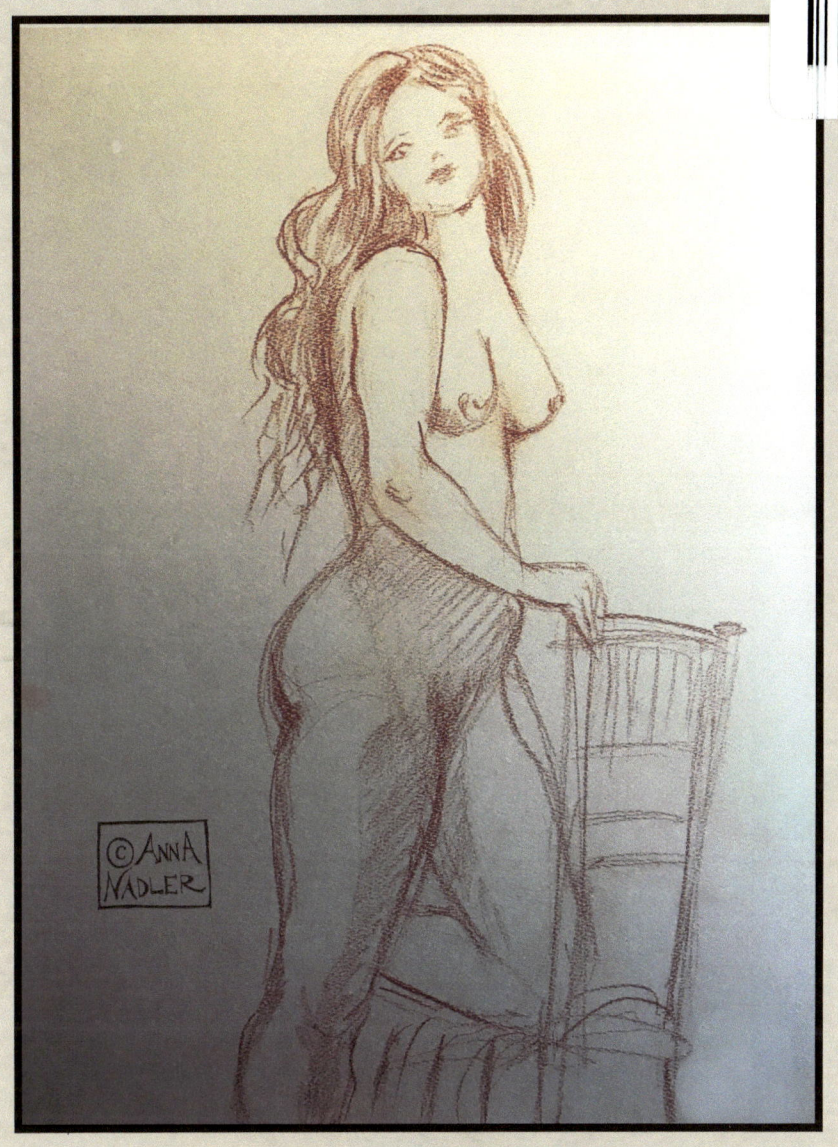

Welcome to "Manhattan Nudes."
Here you will see a collection of life drawings done on location at different art studios in New York City, over a span of about five years. The mediums used in the drawings include, pencil, pen, watercolor, marker and pastel. I hope you enjoy this book!
Thank you!

Anna

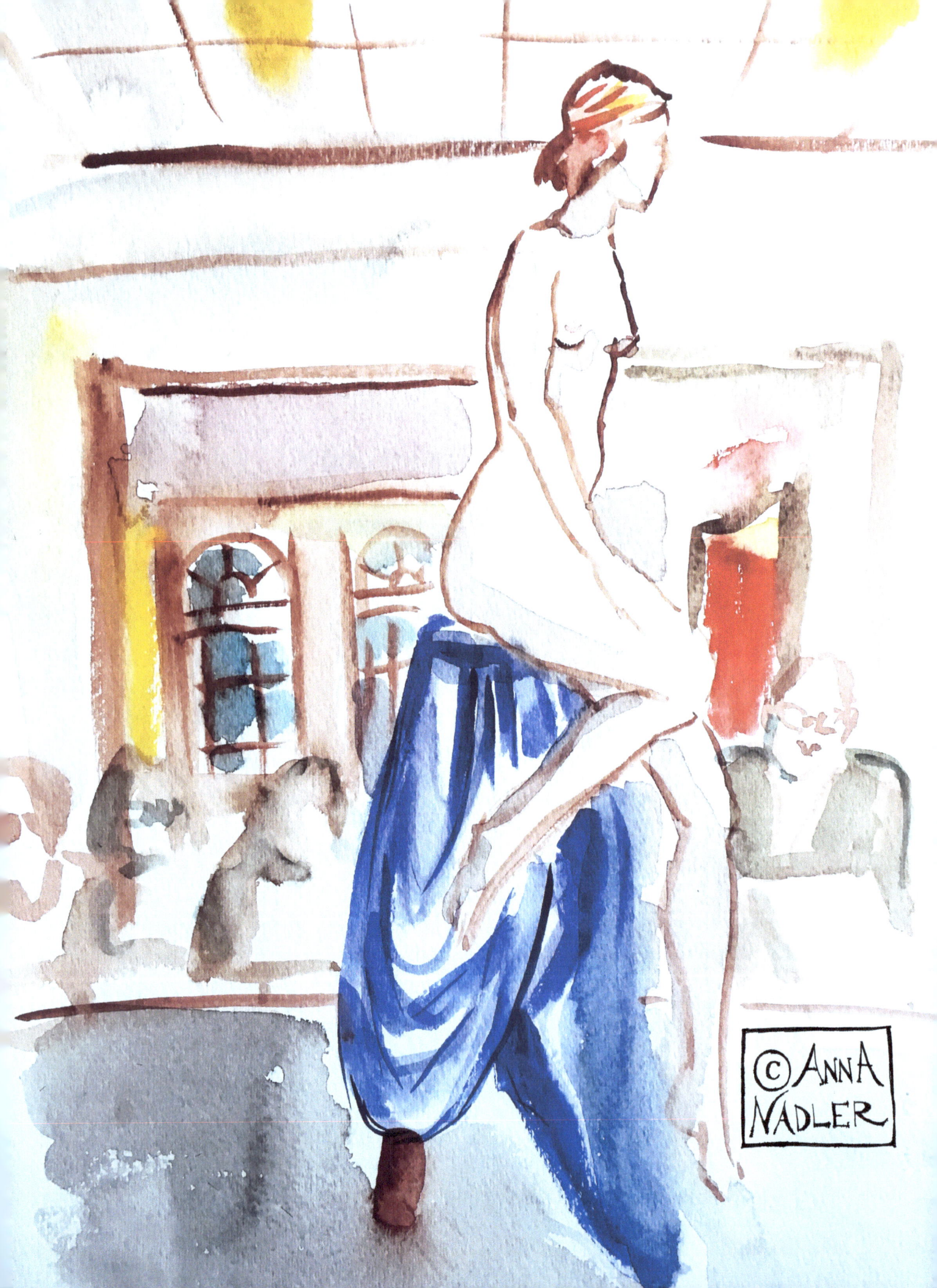

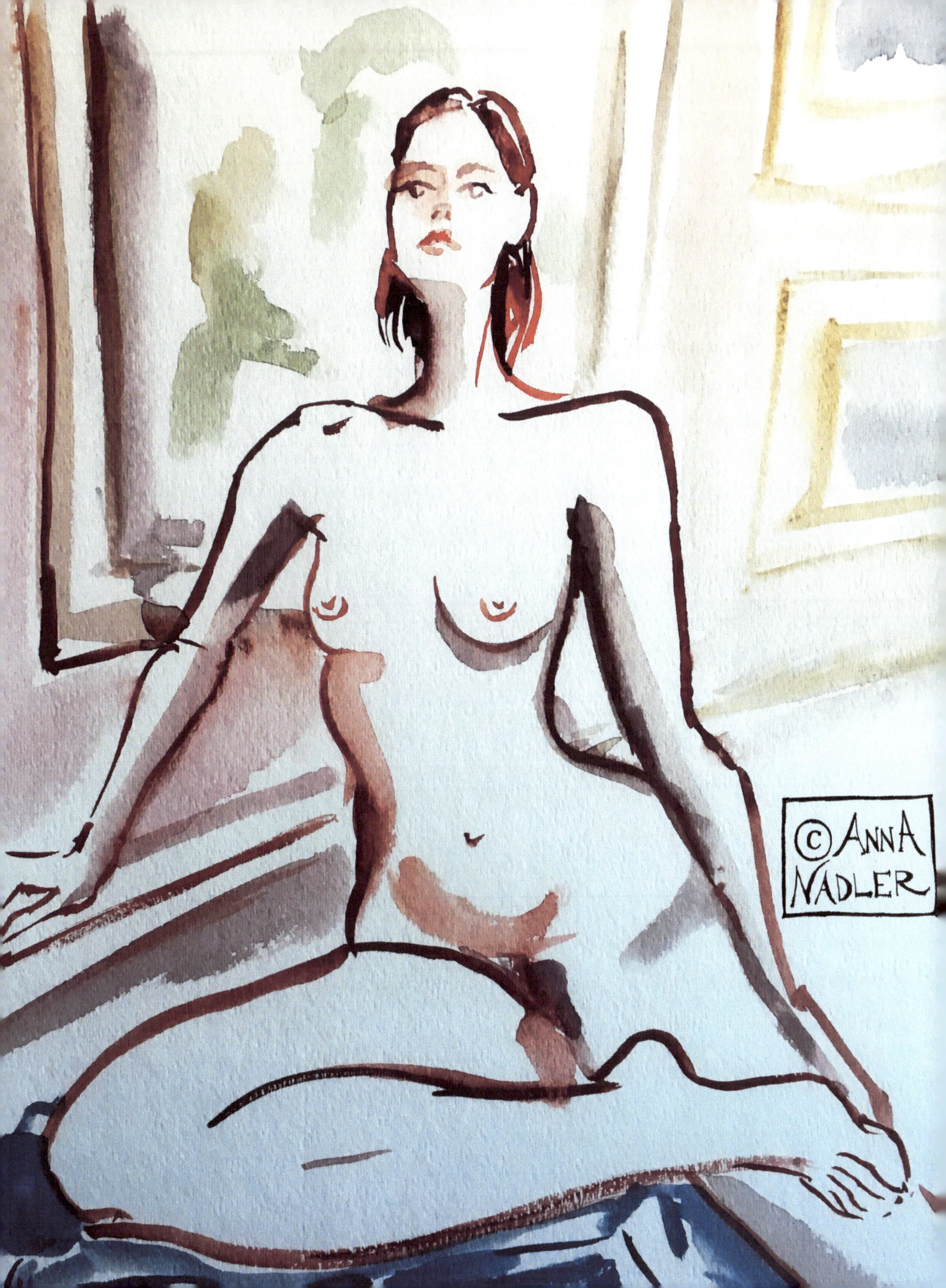

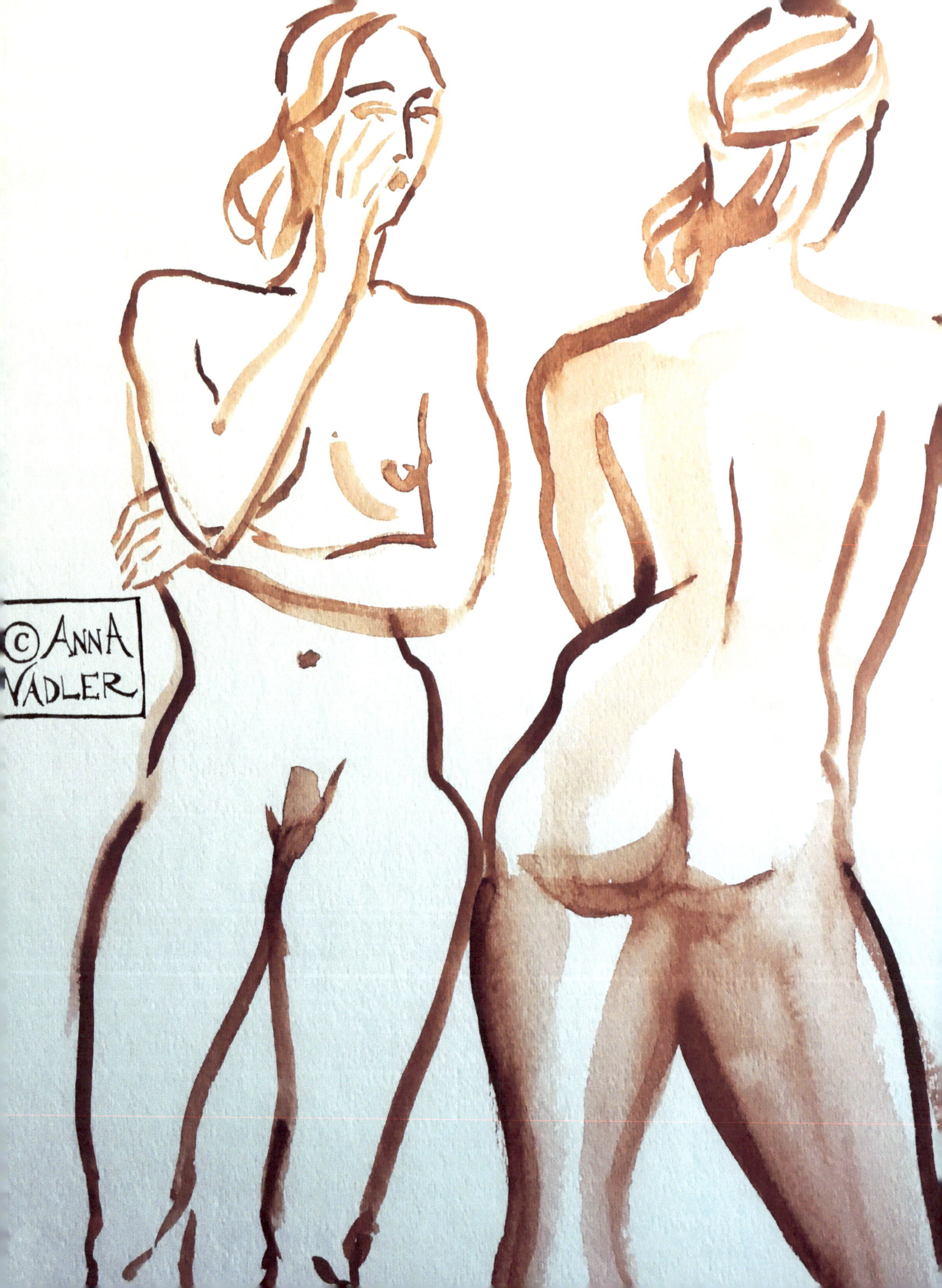

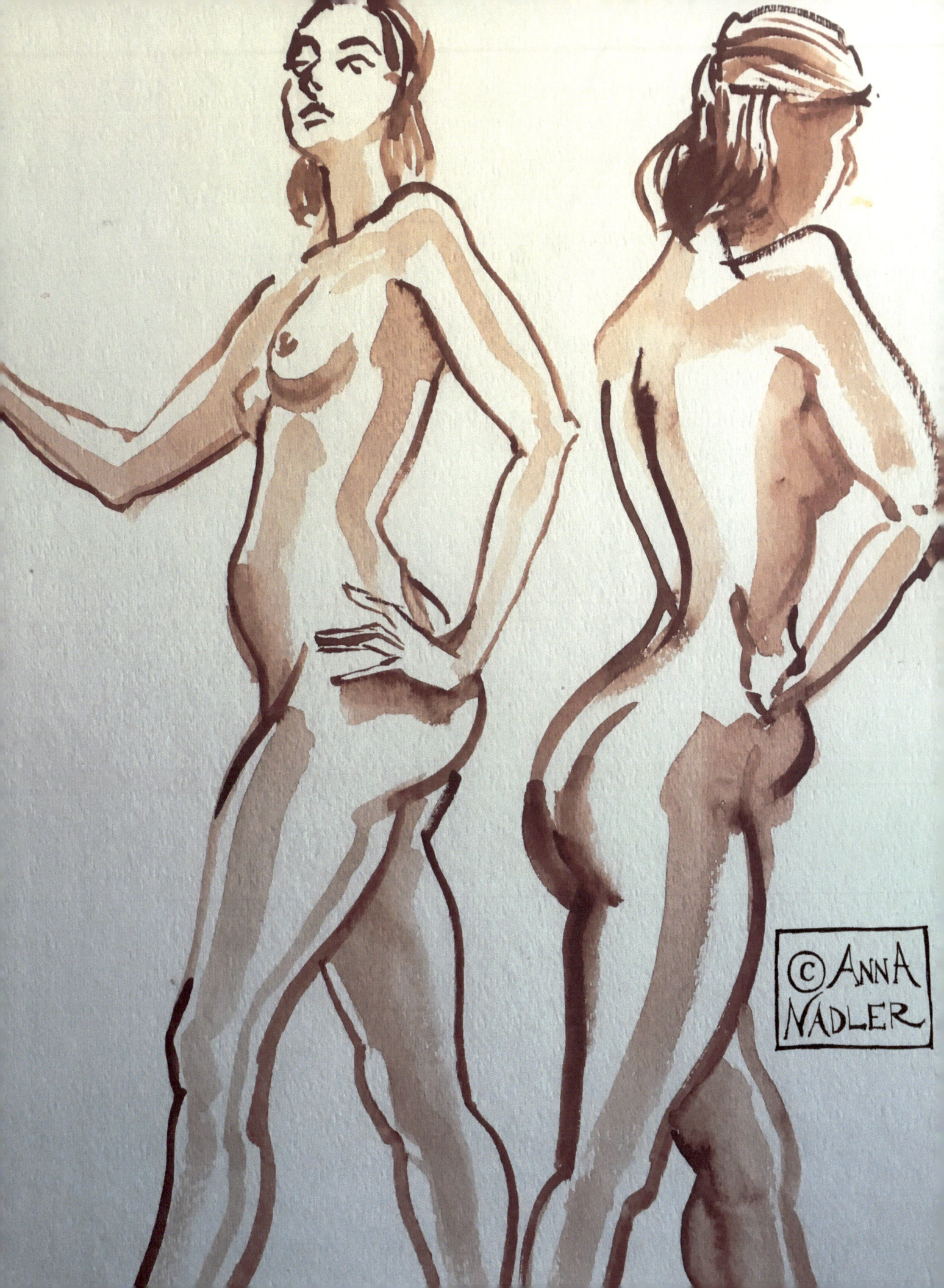

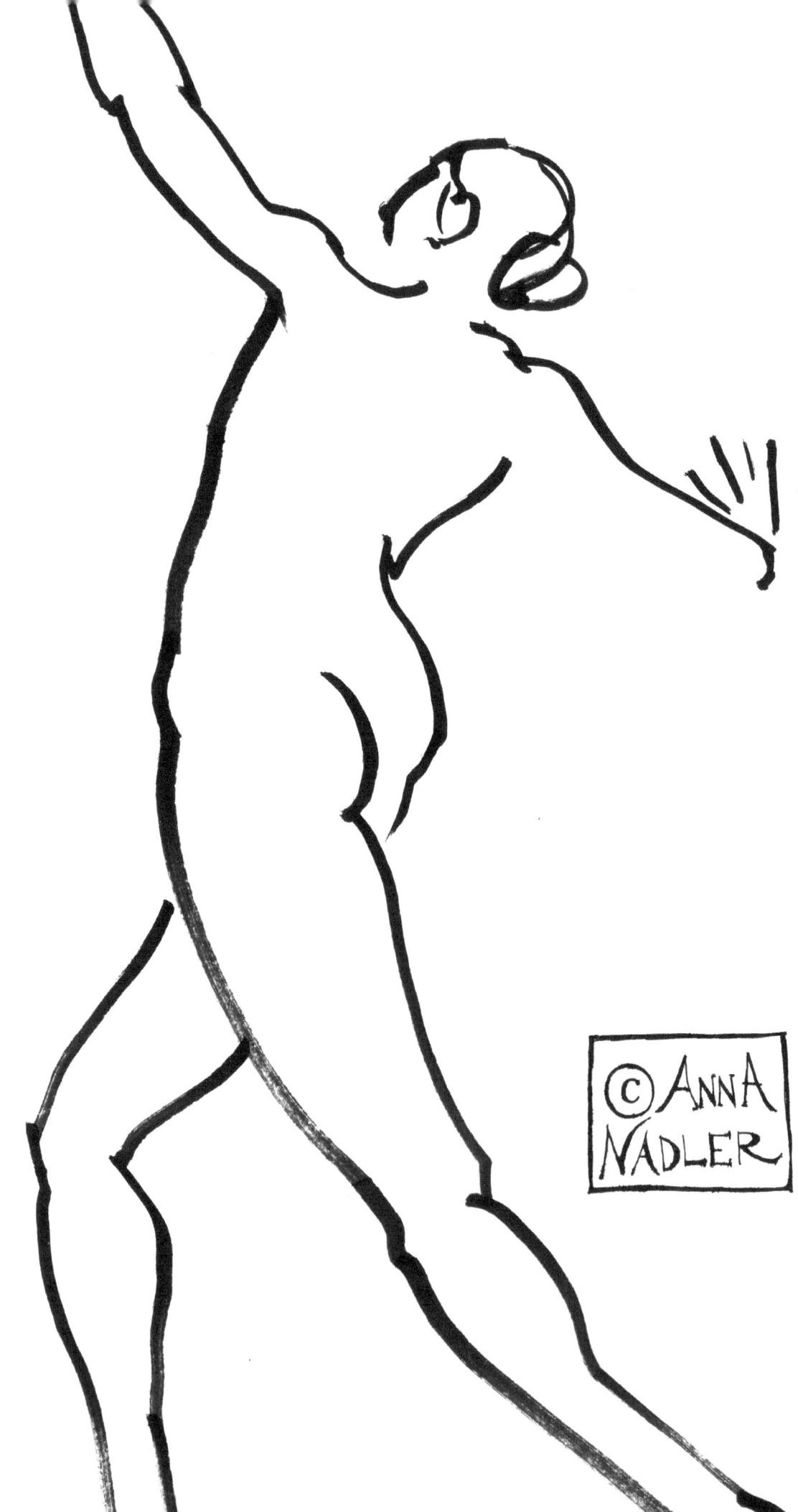

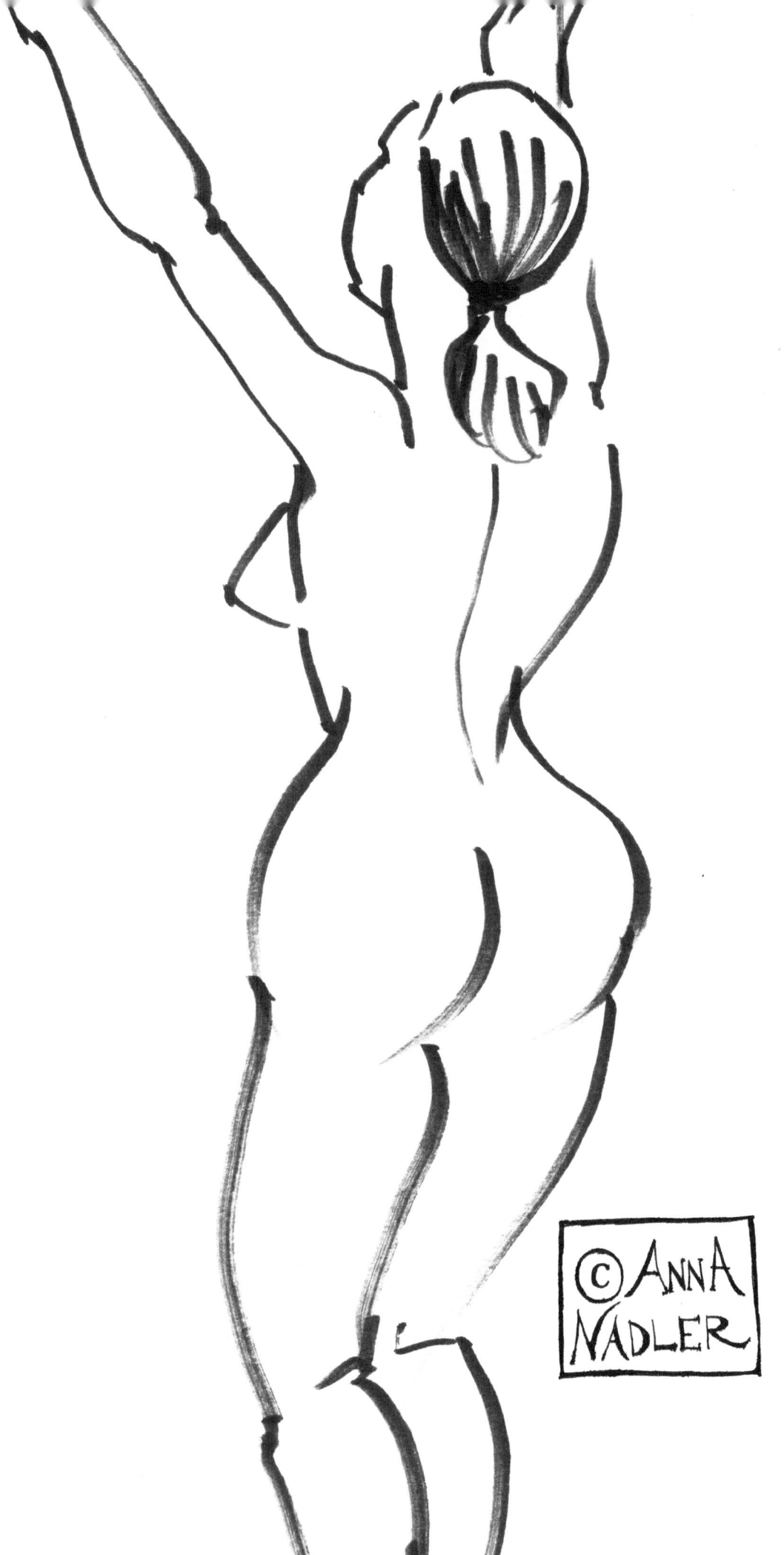

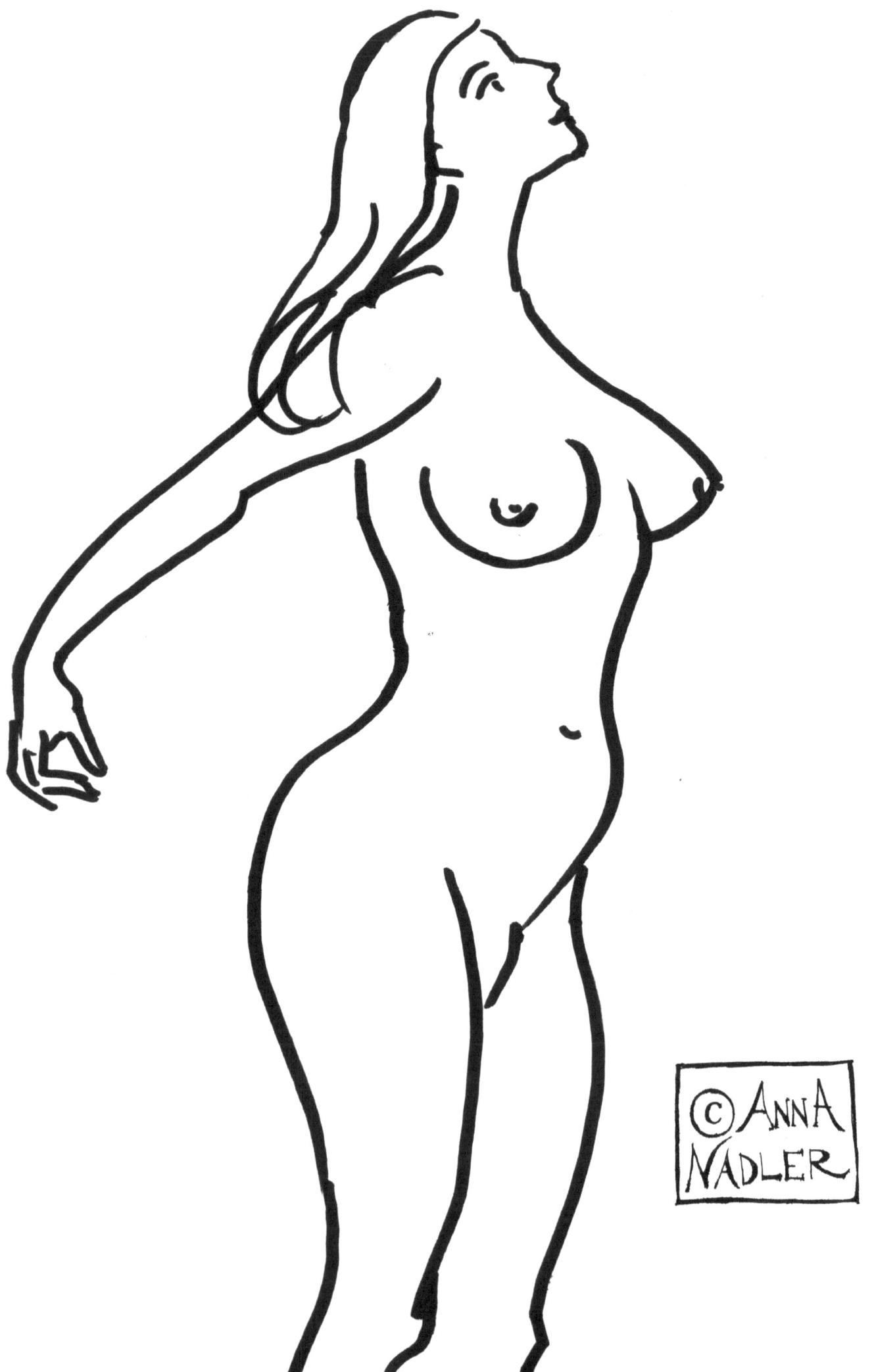

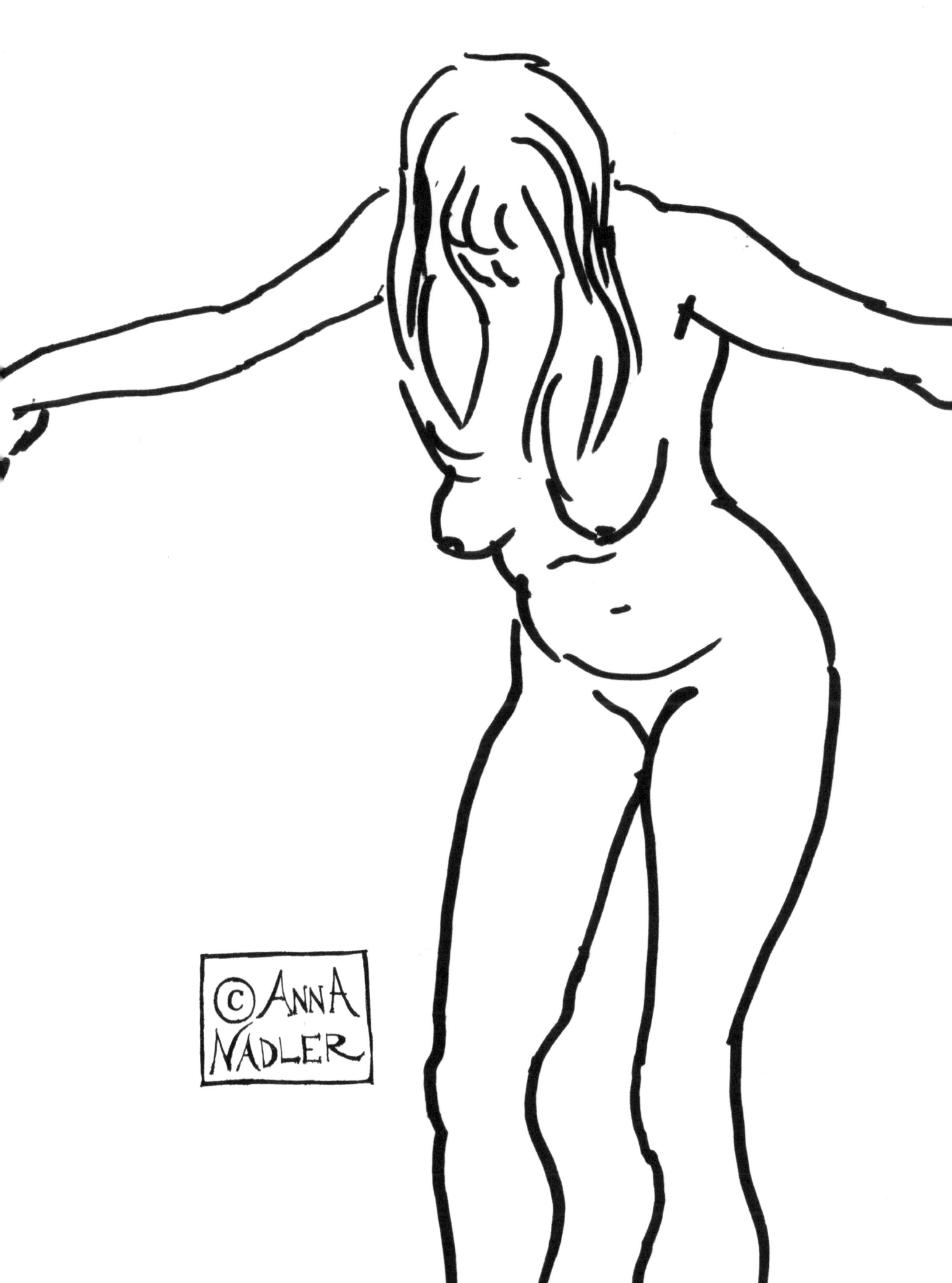

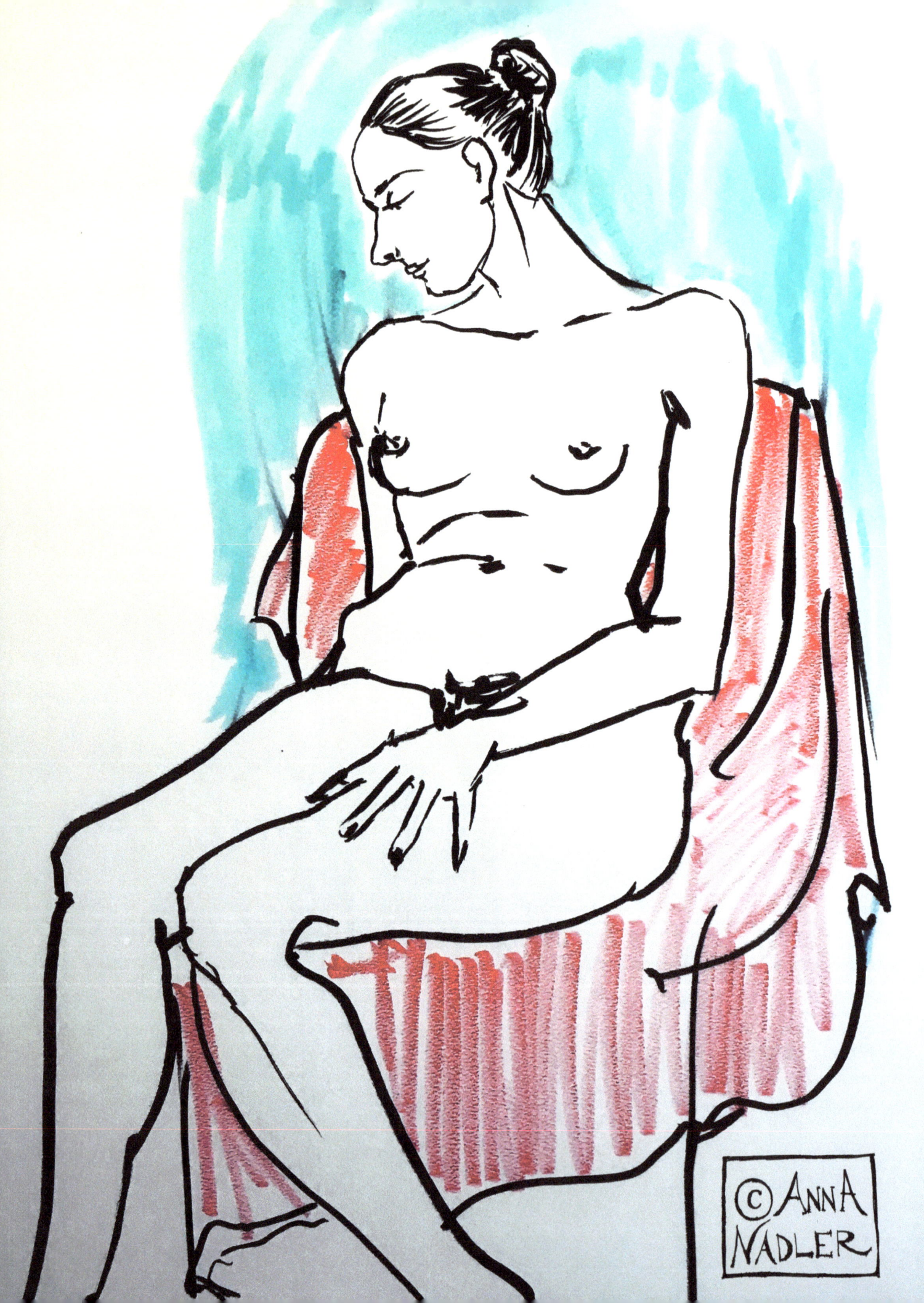

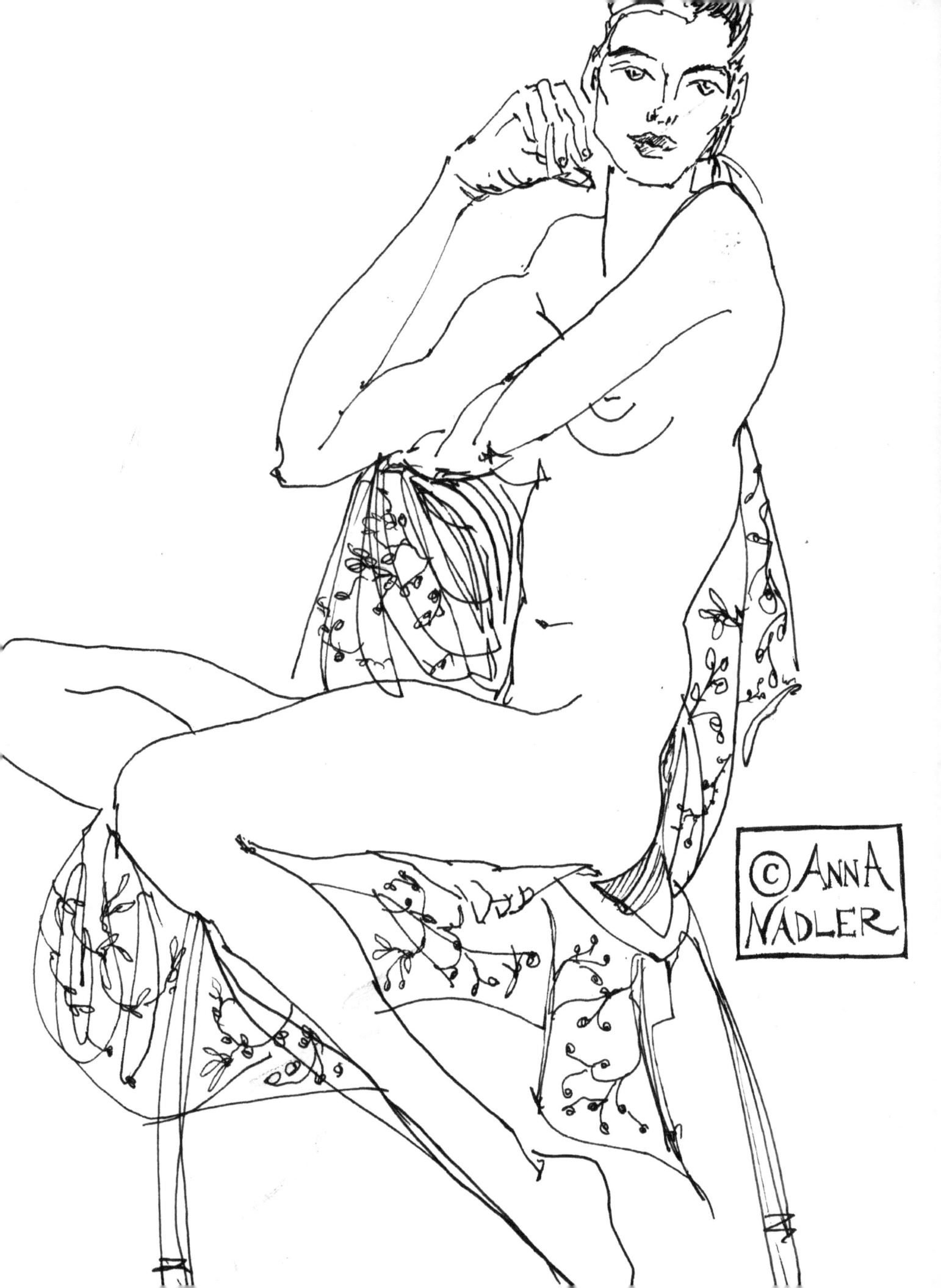

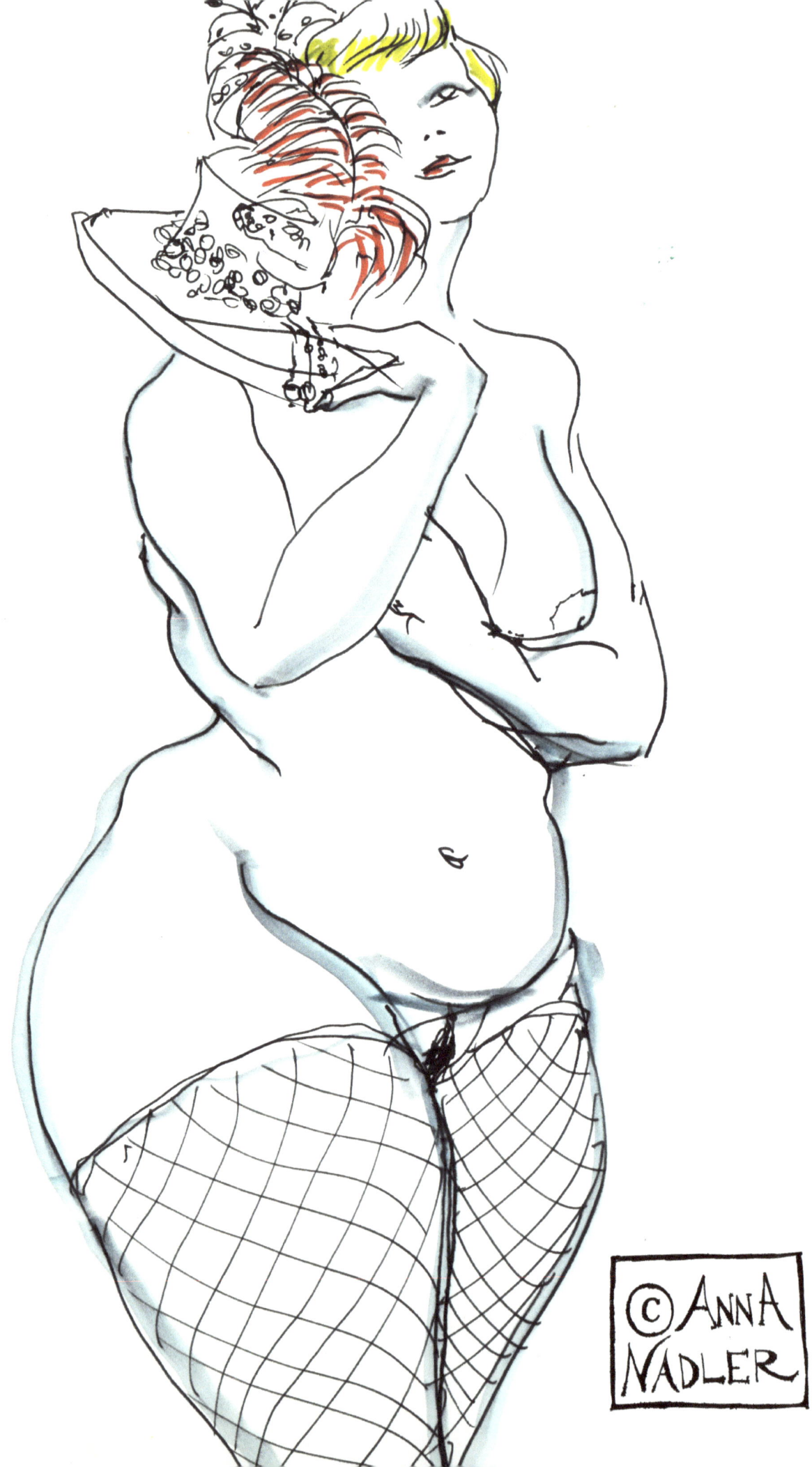

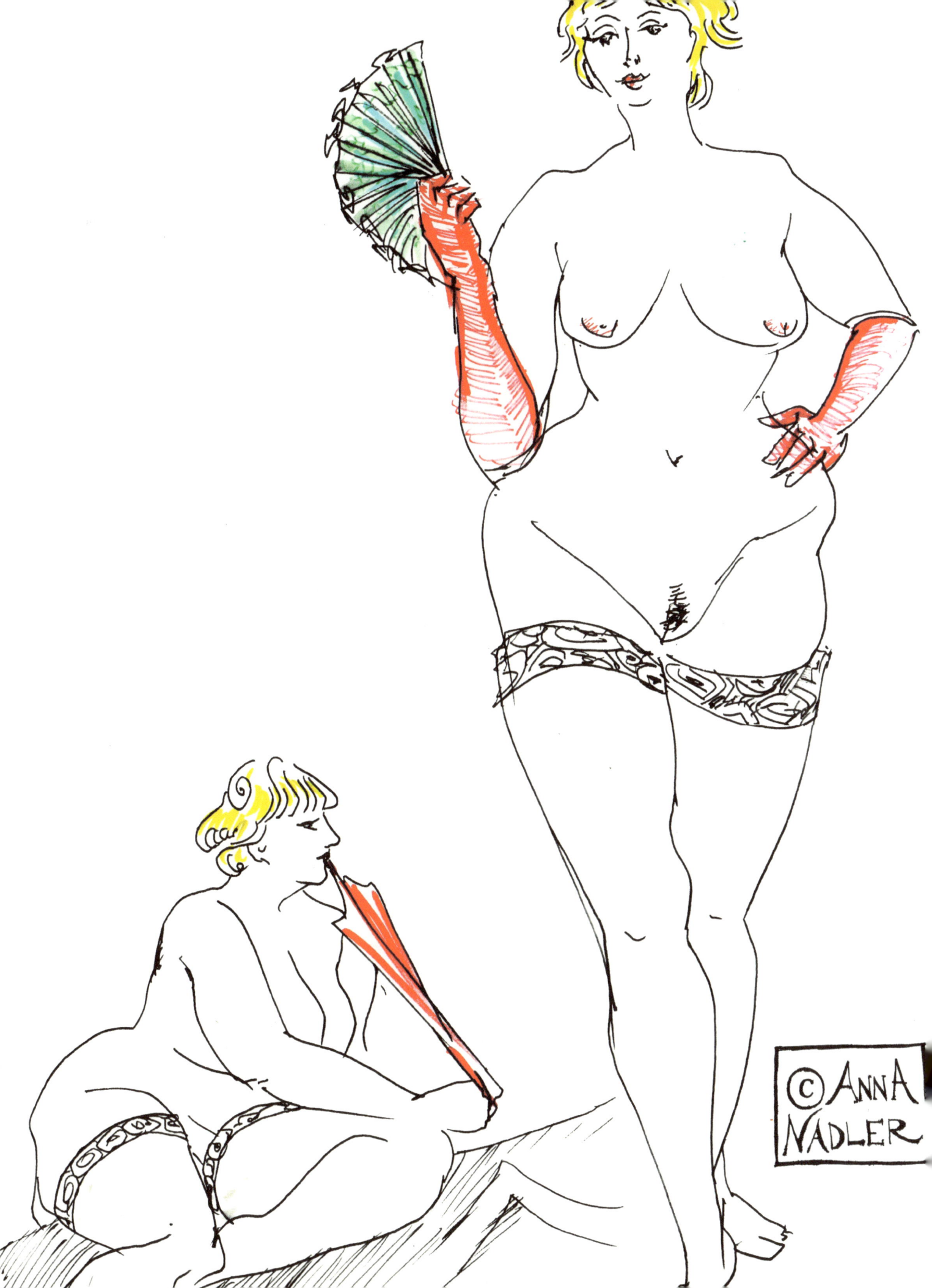

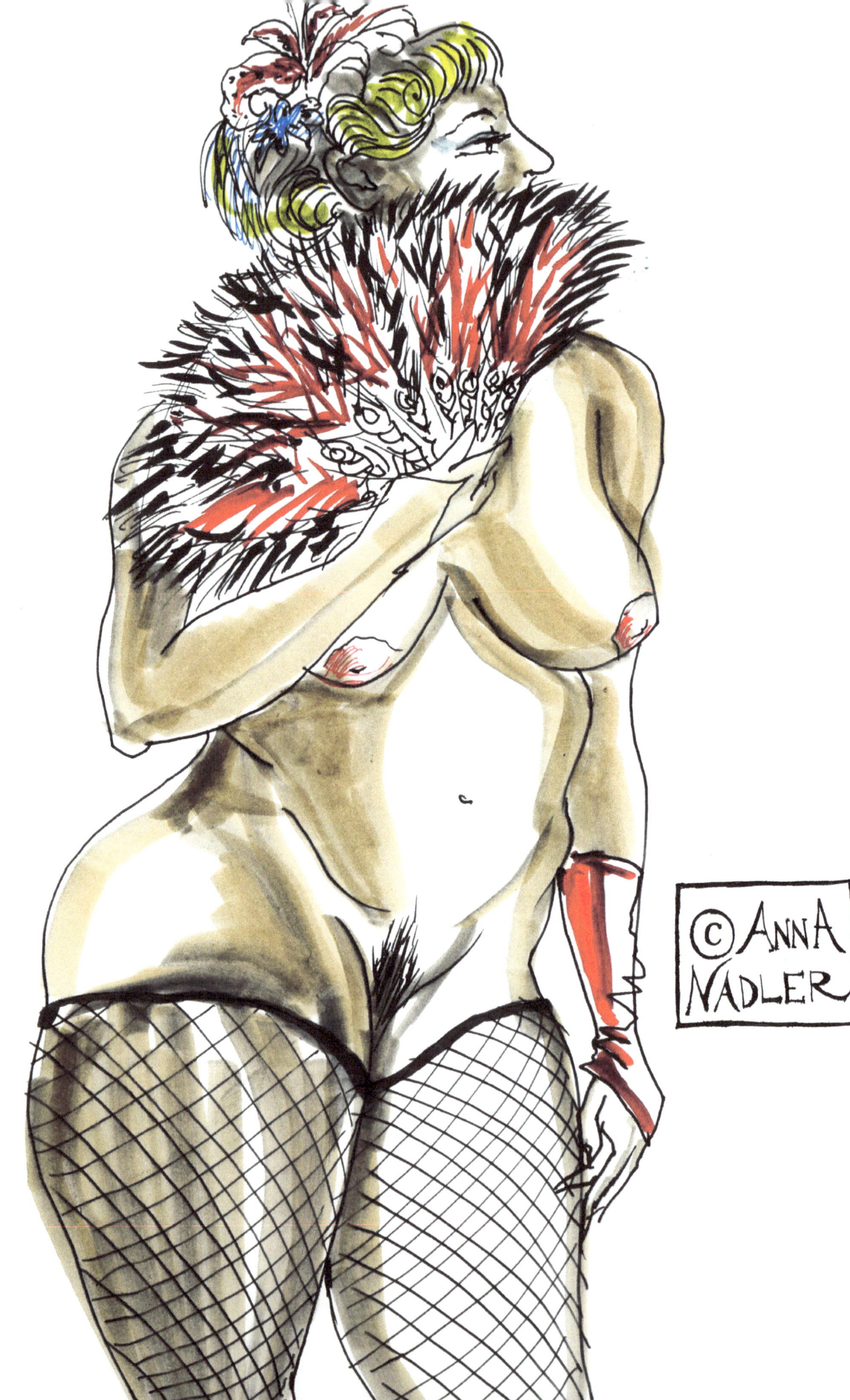

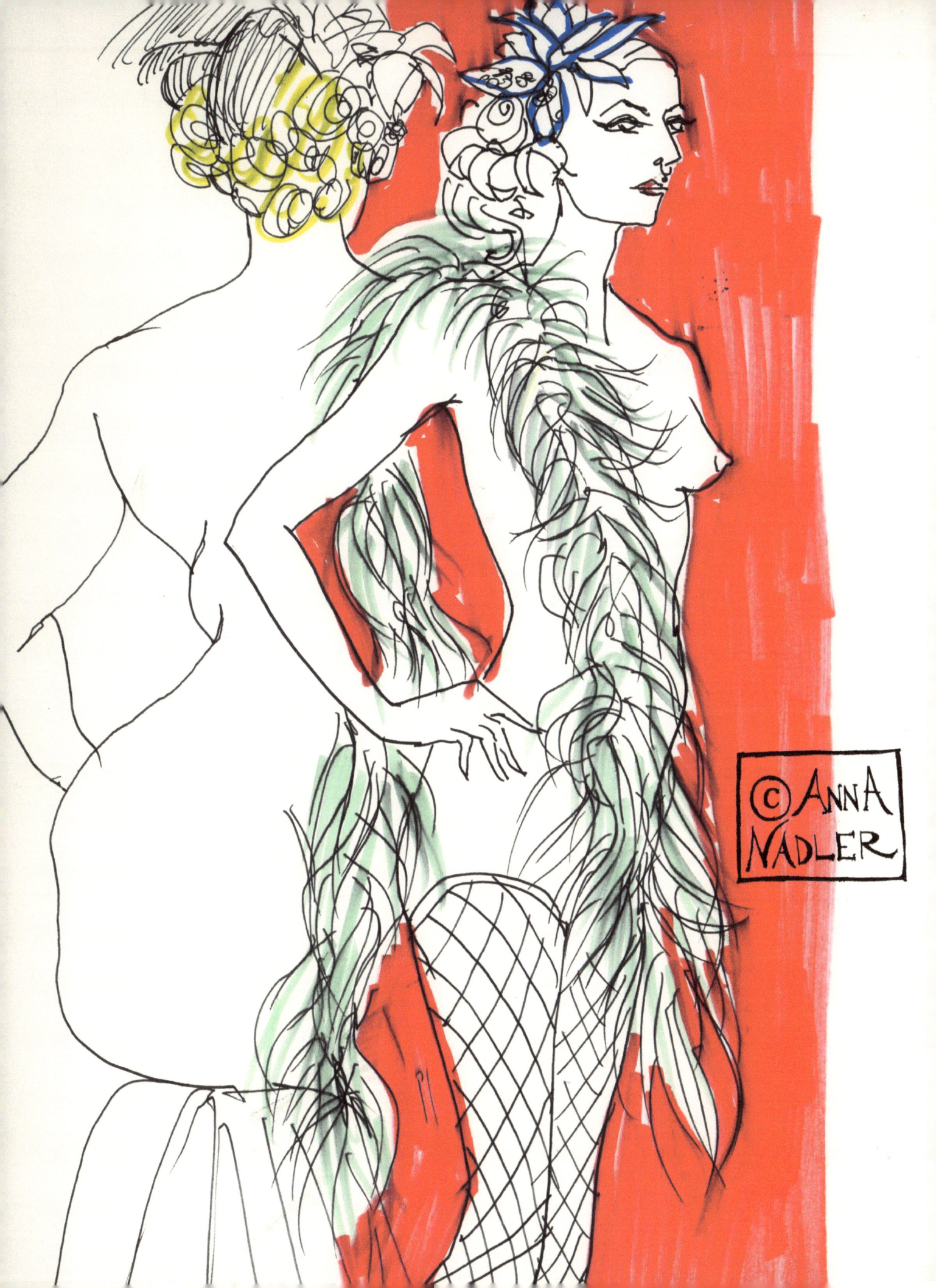

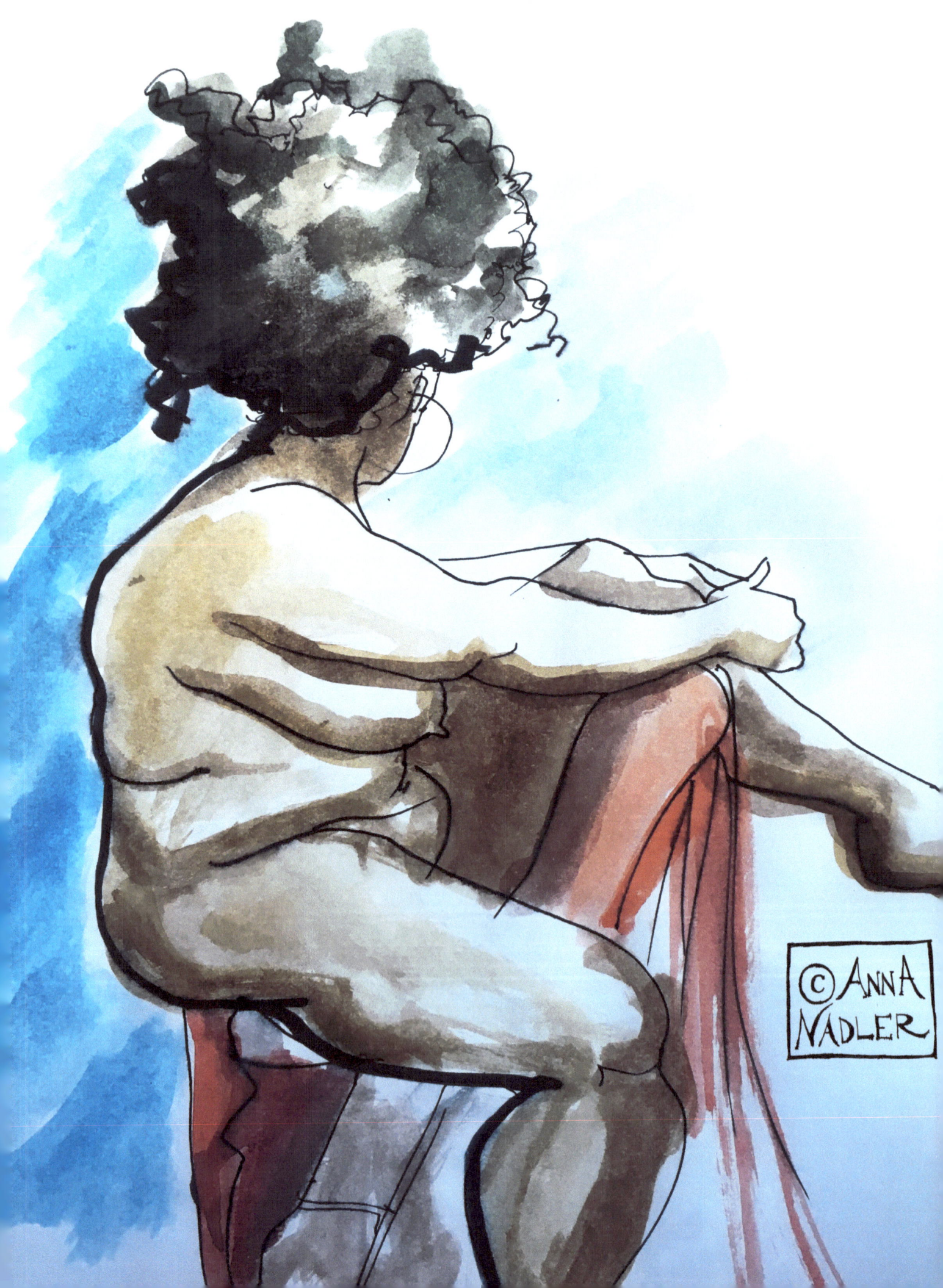

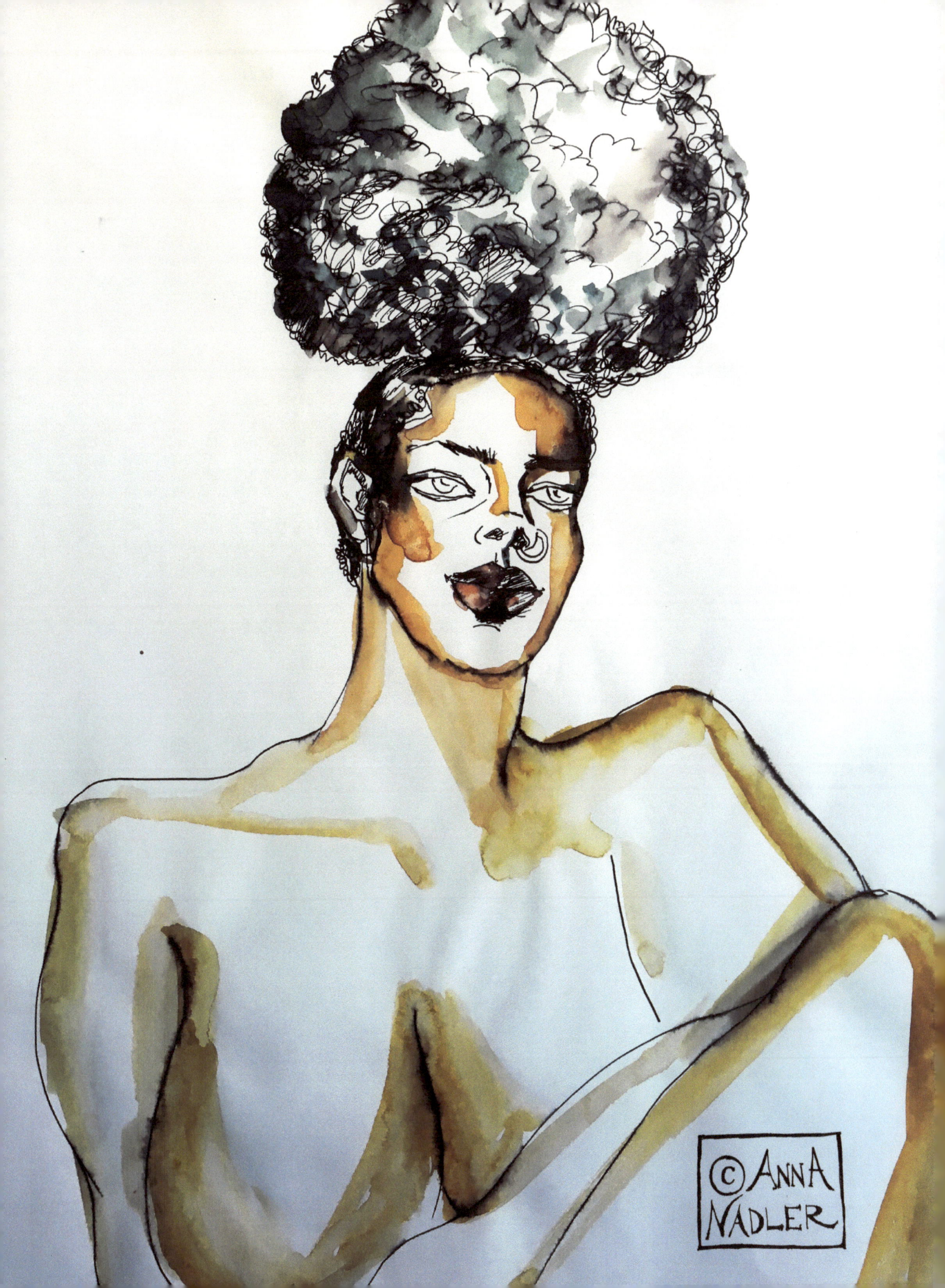

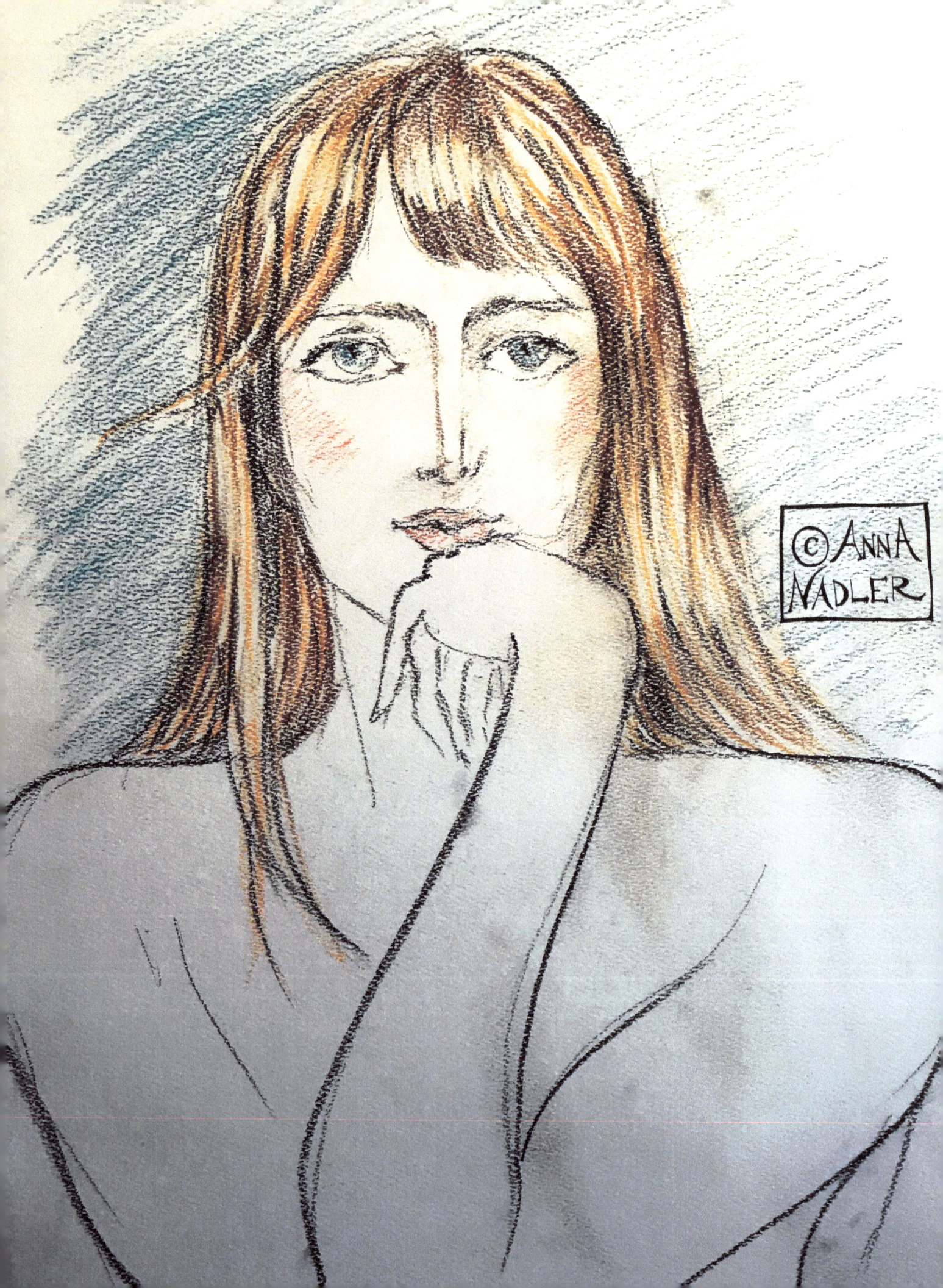

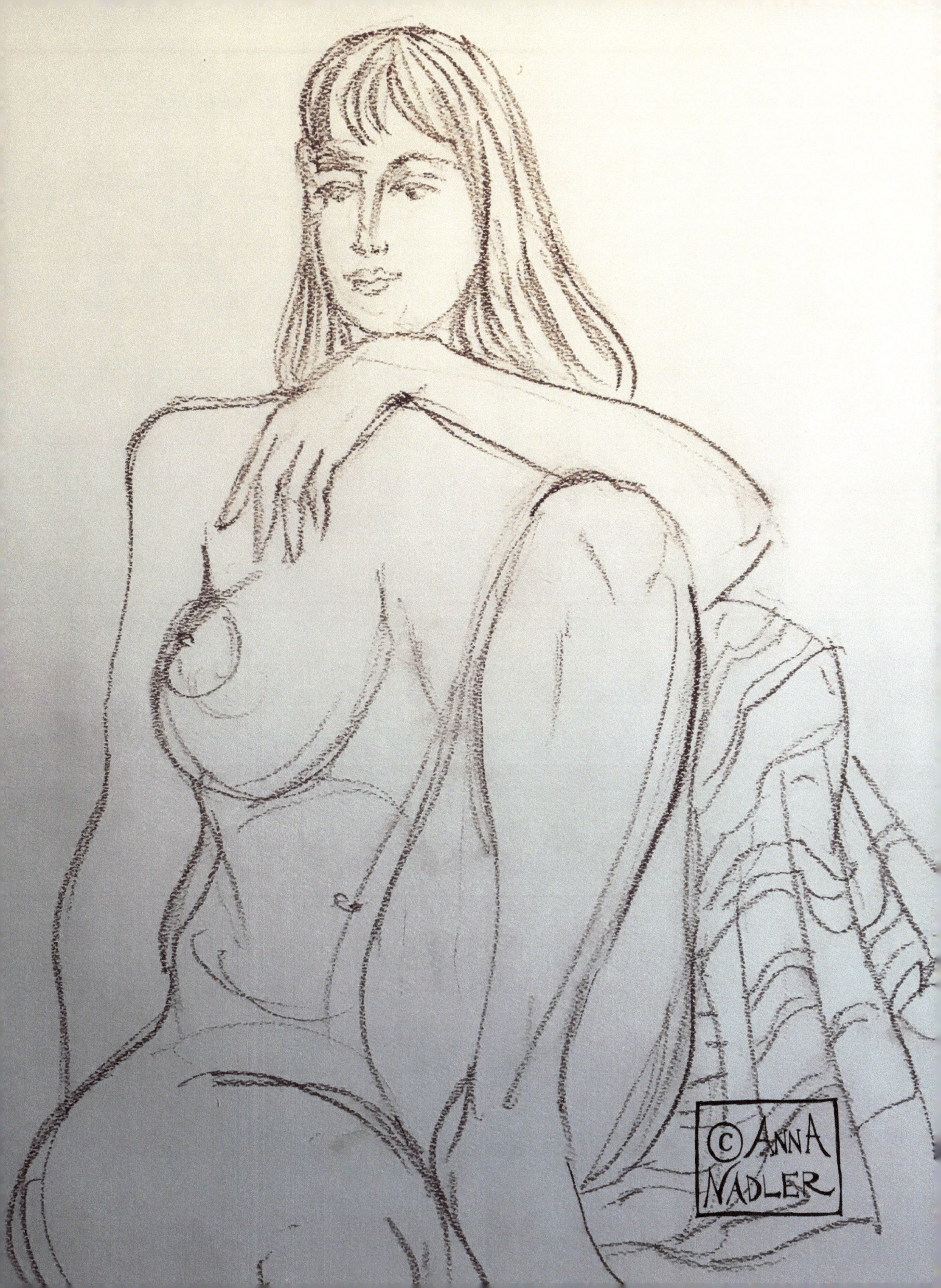

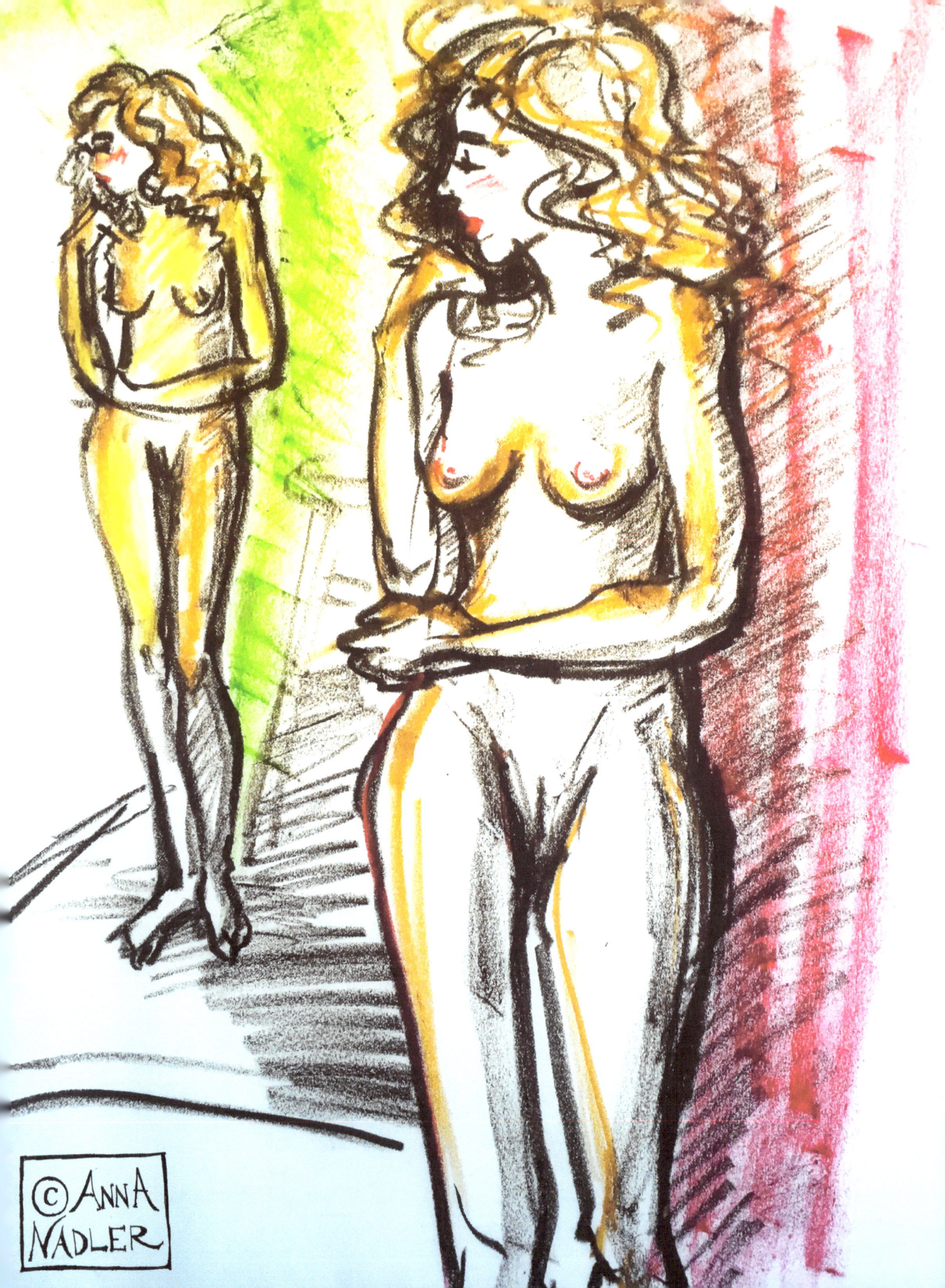

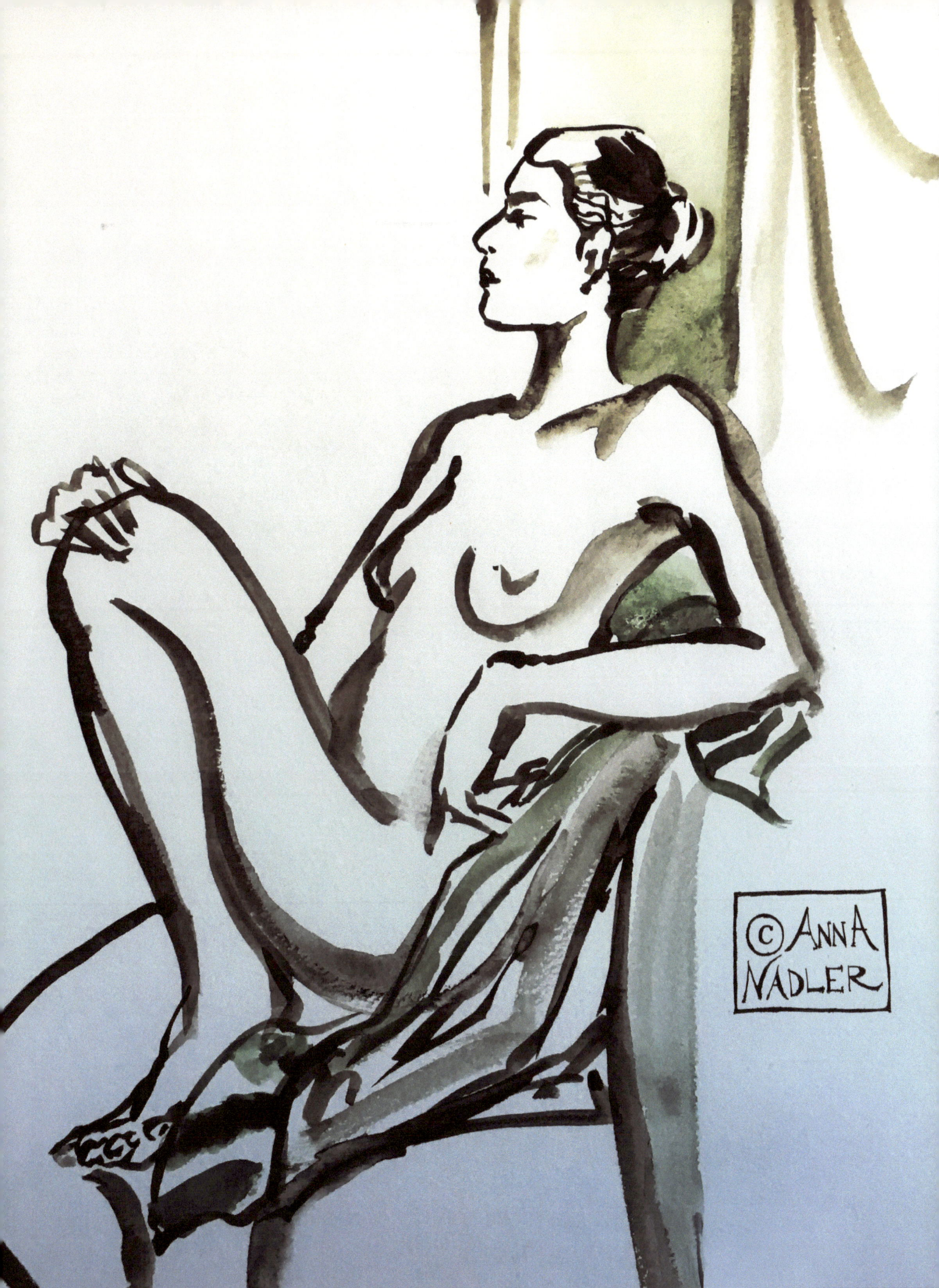

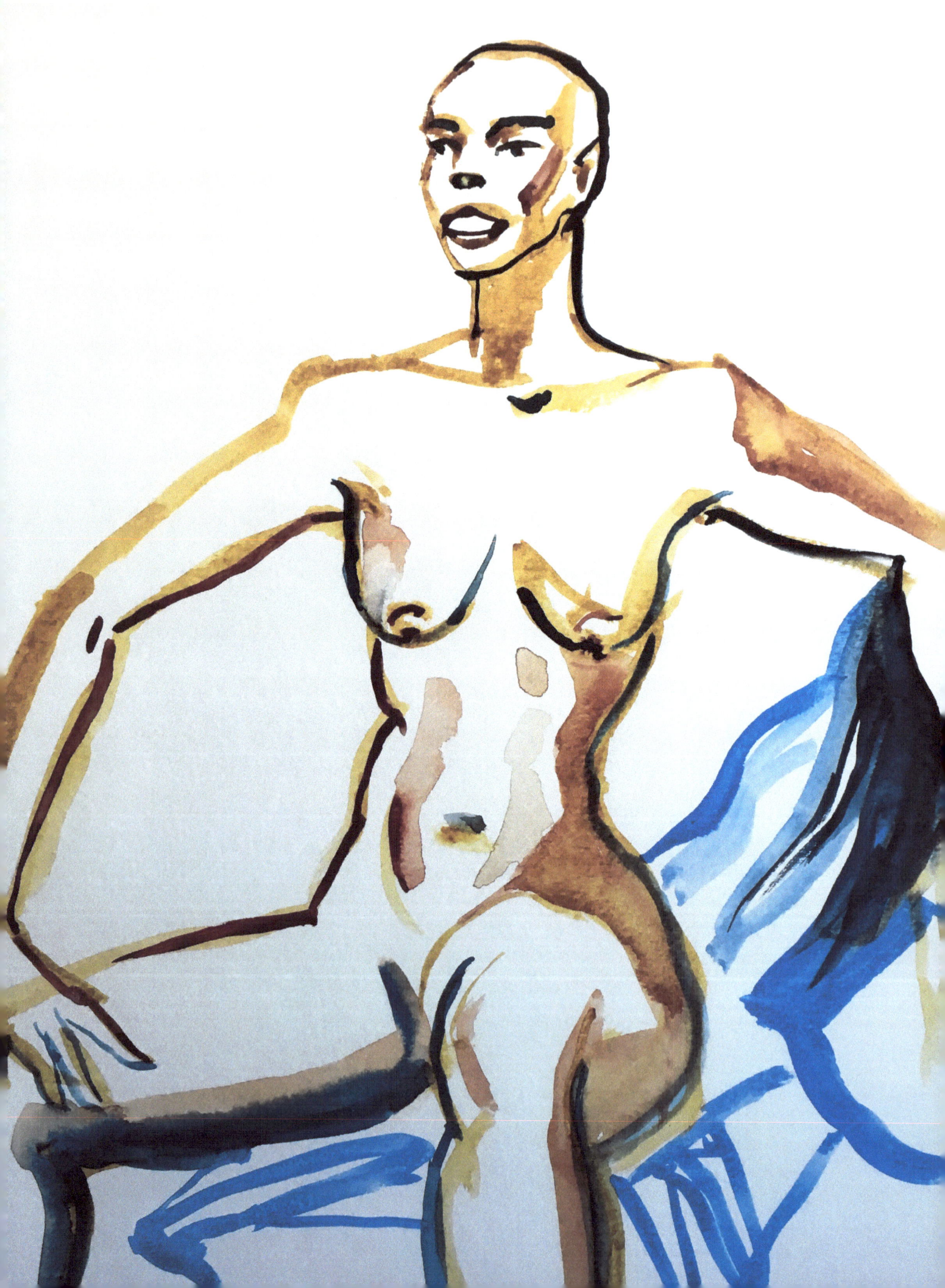

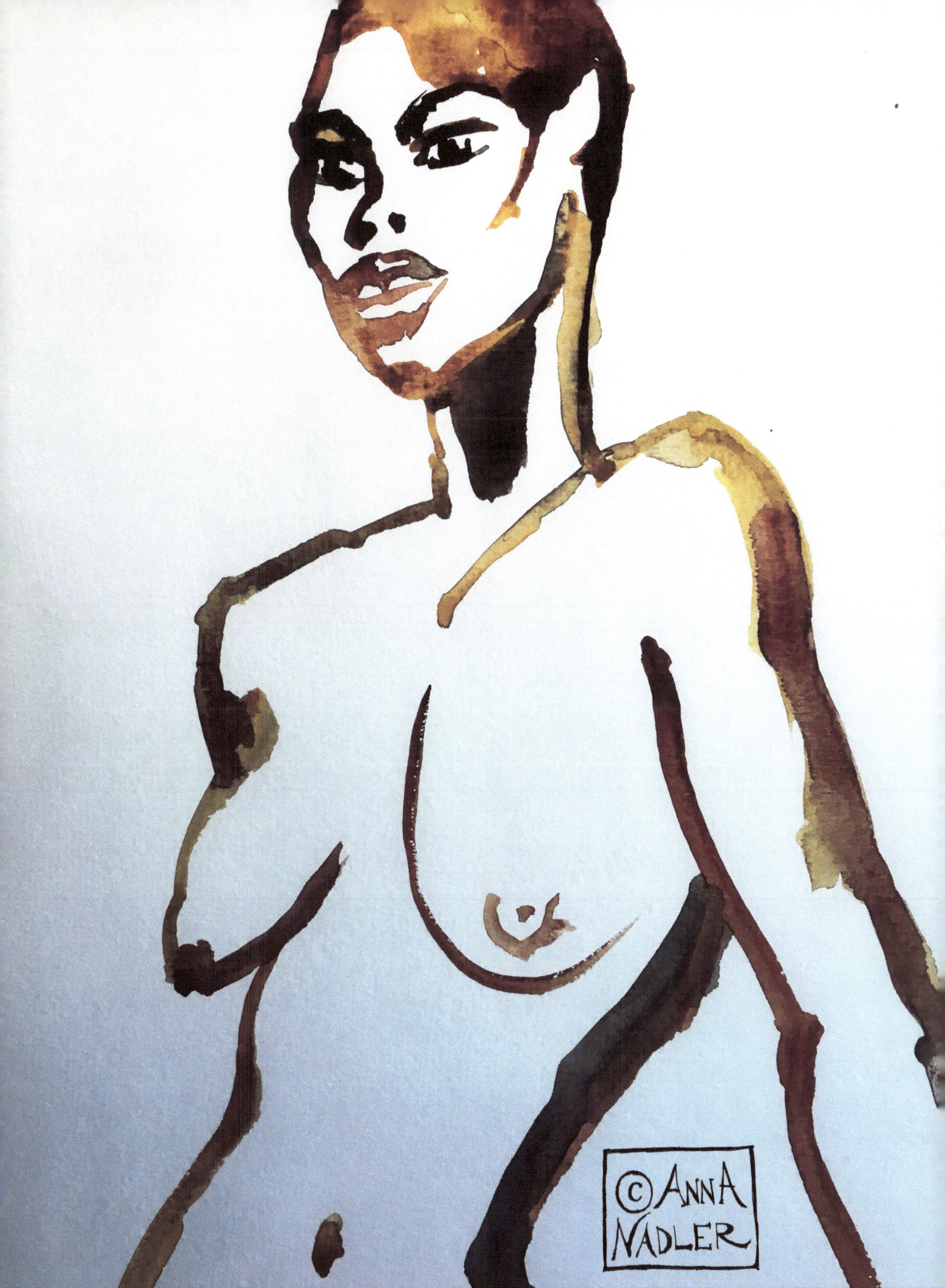

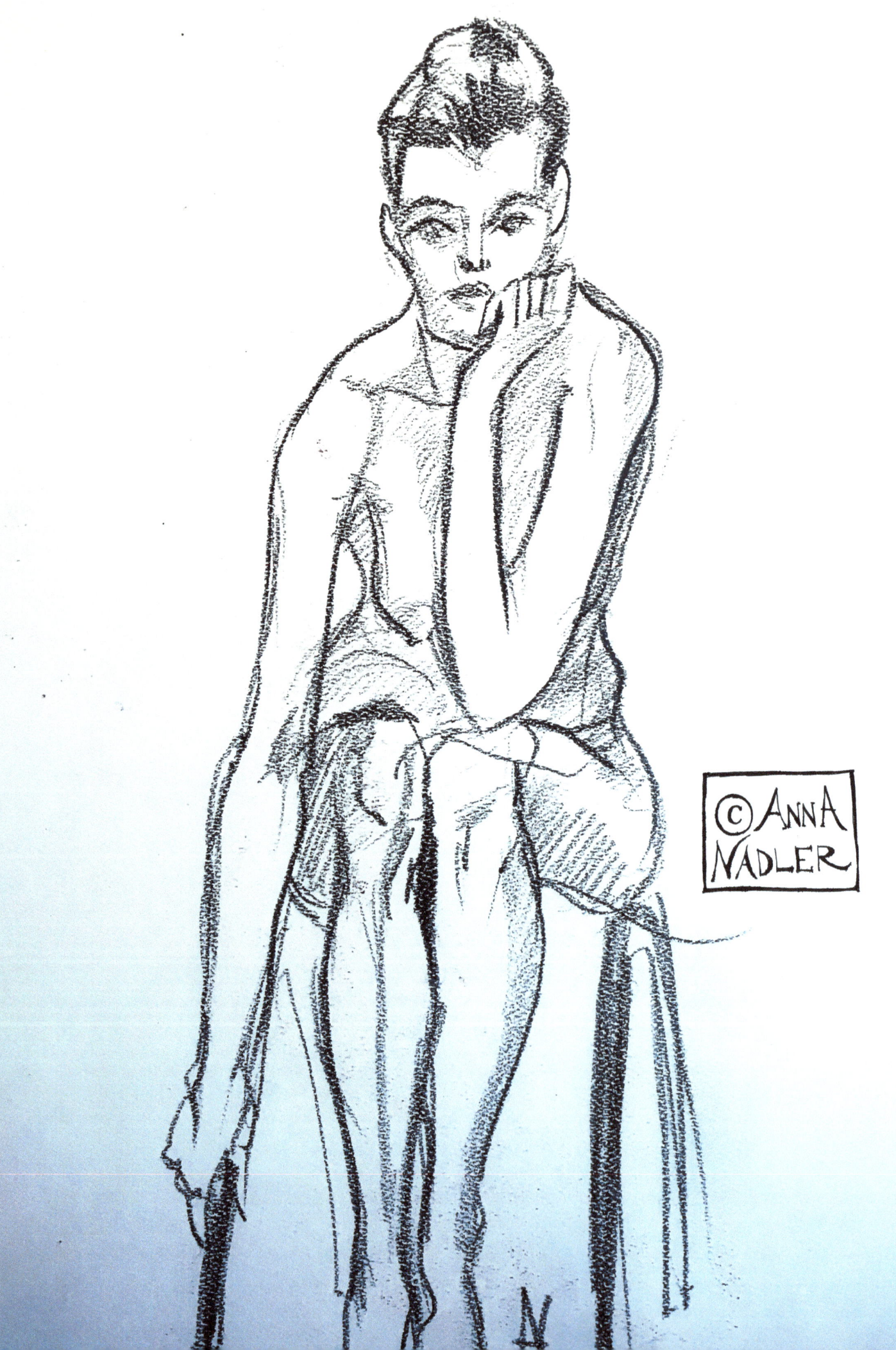

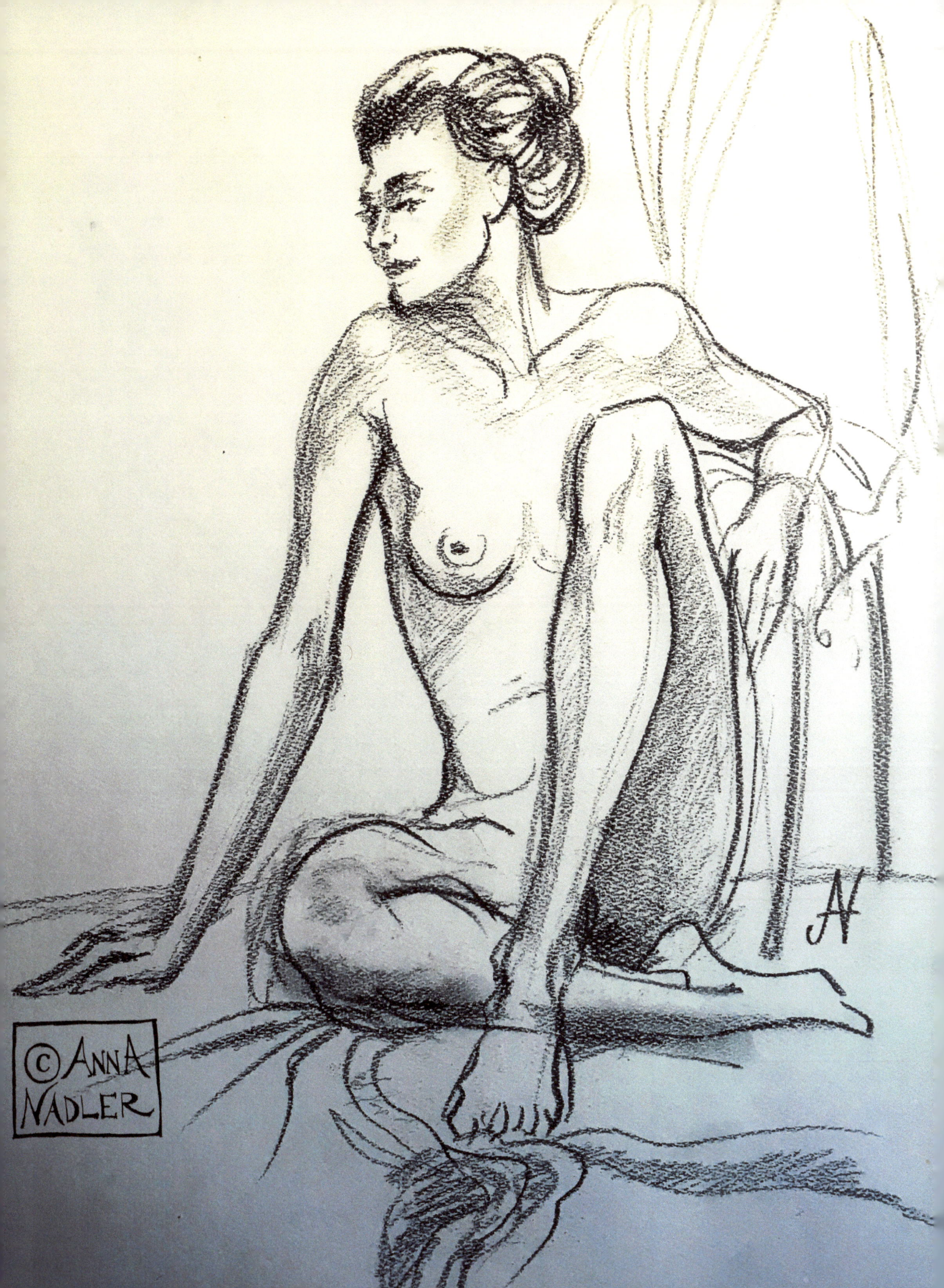

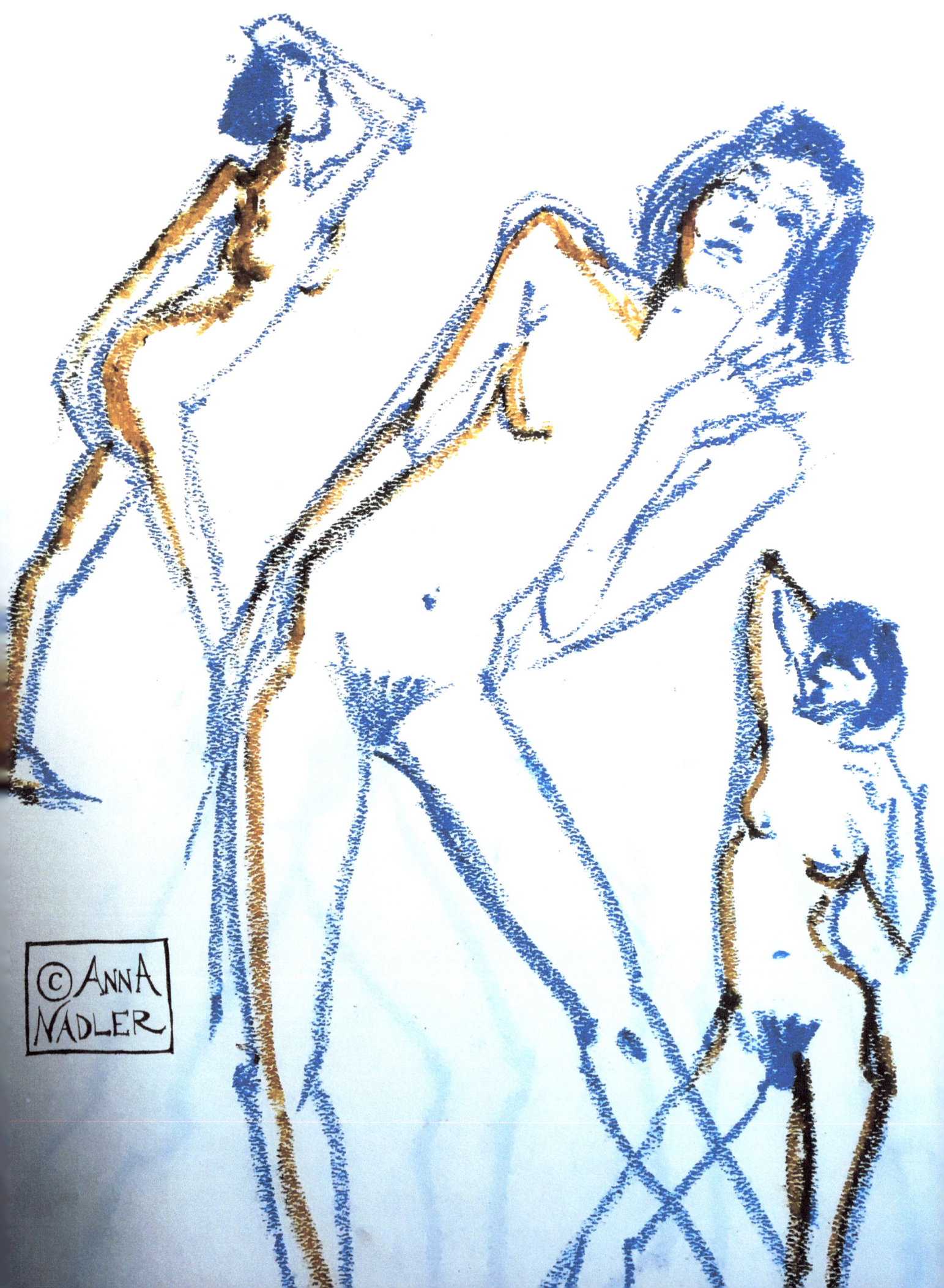

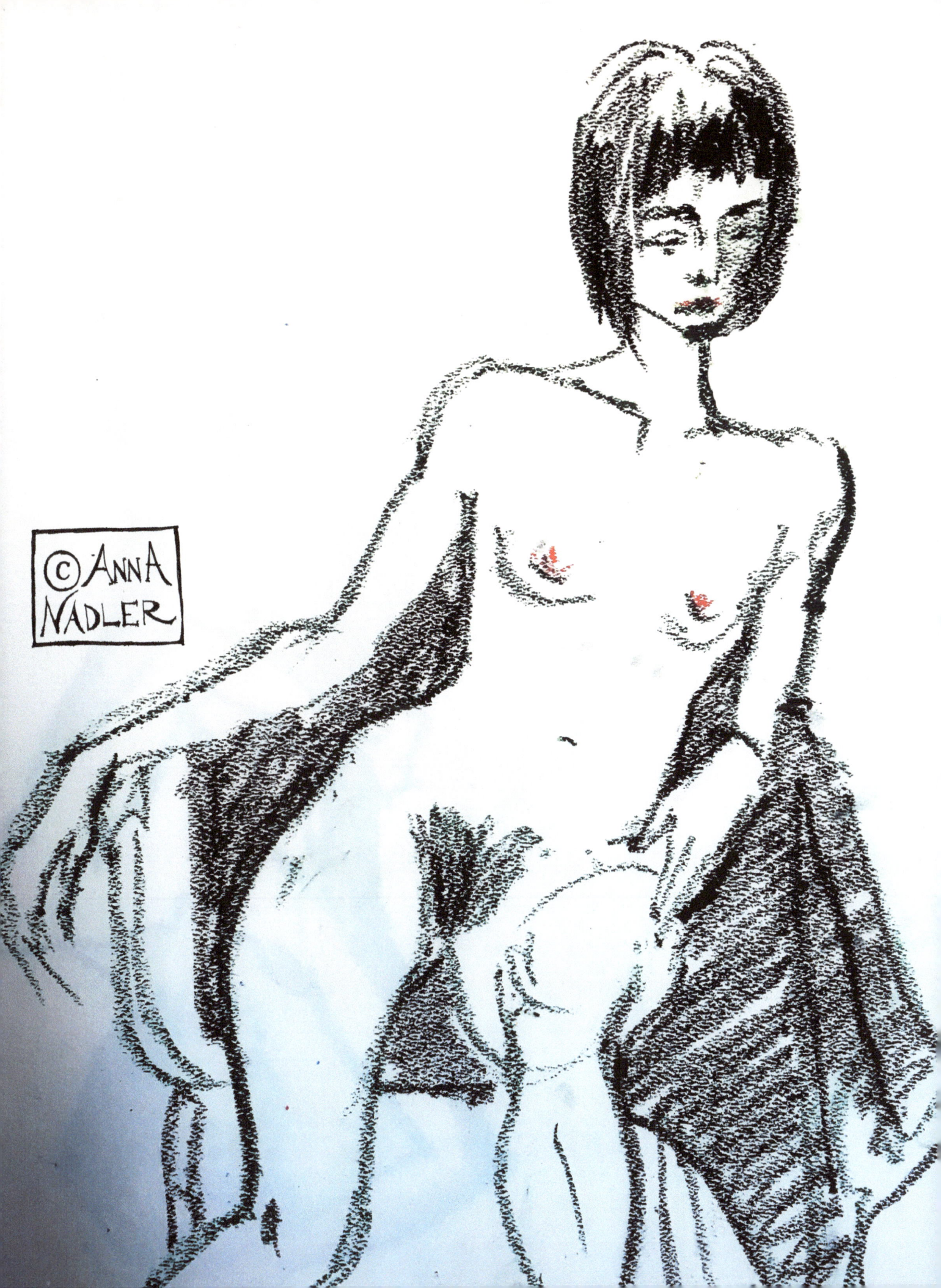

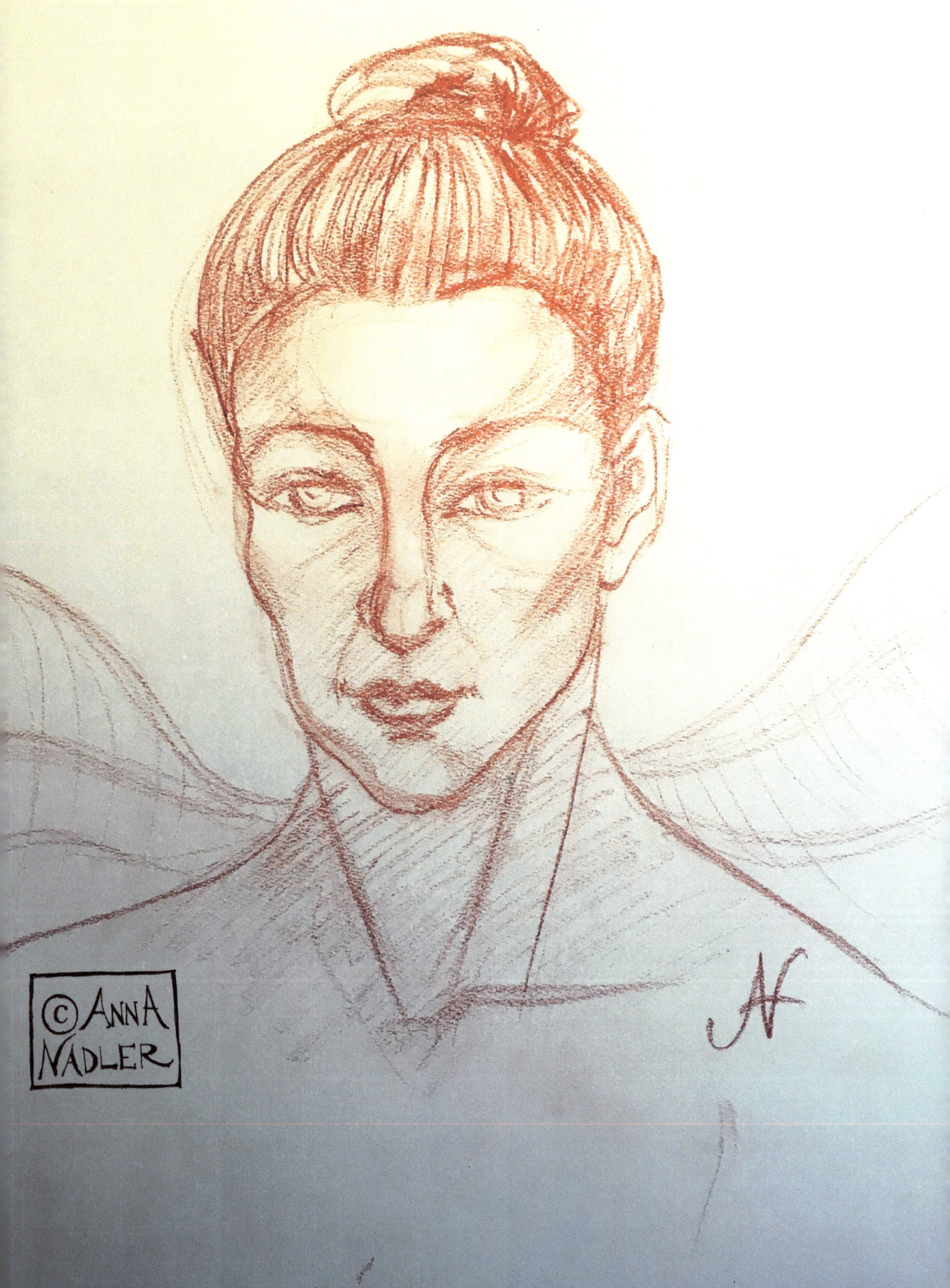

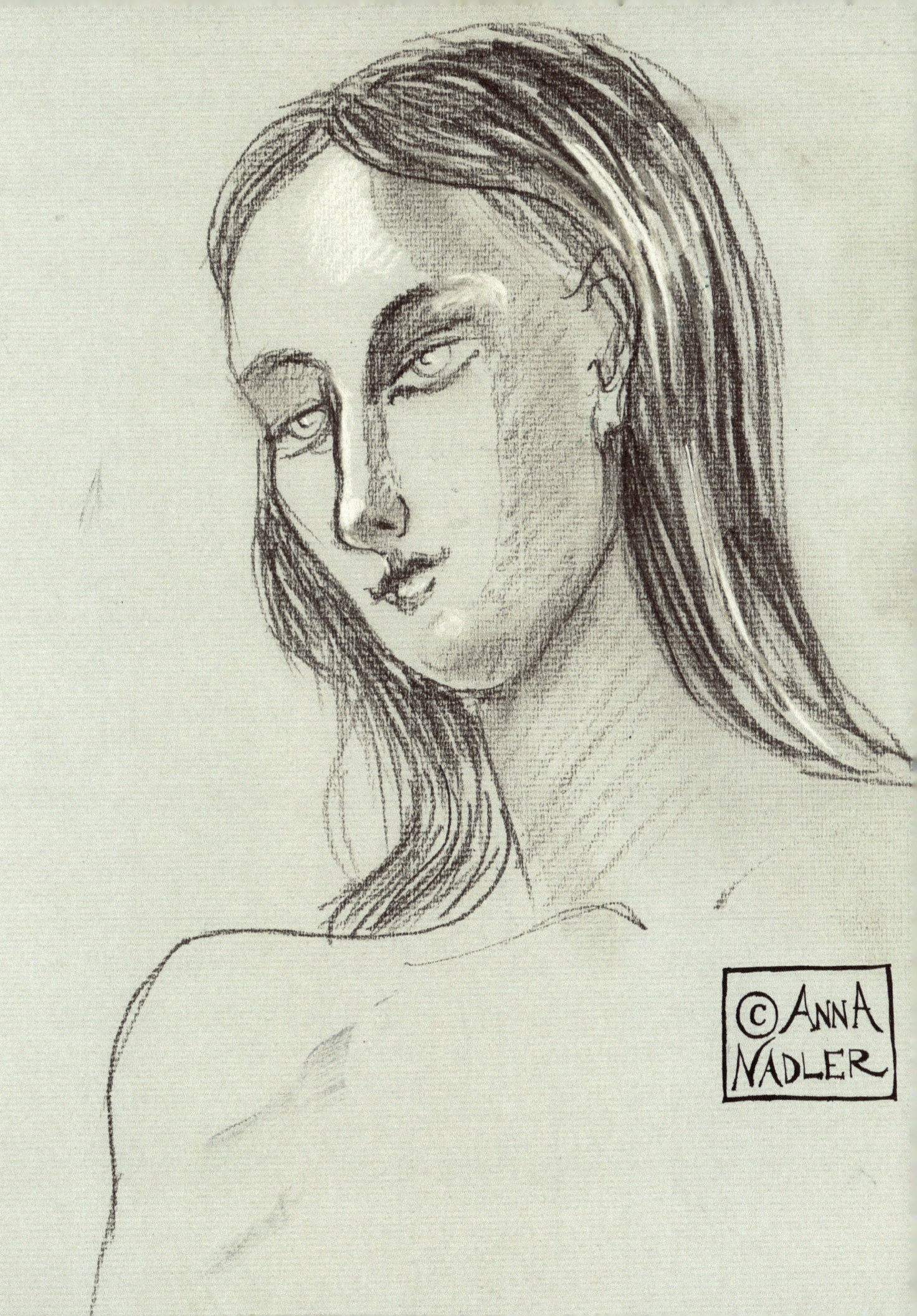

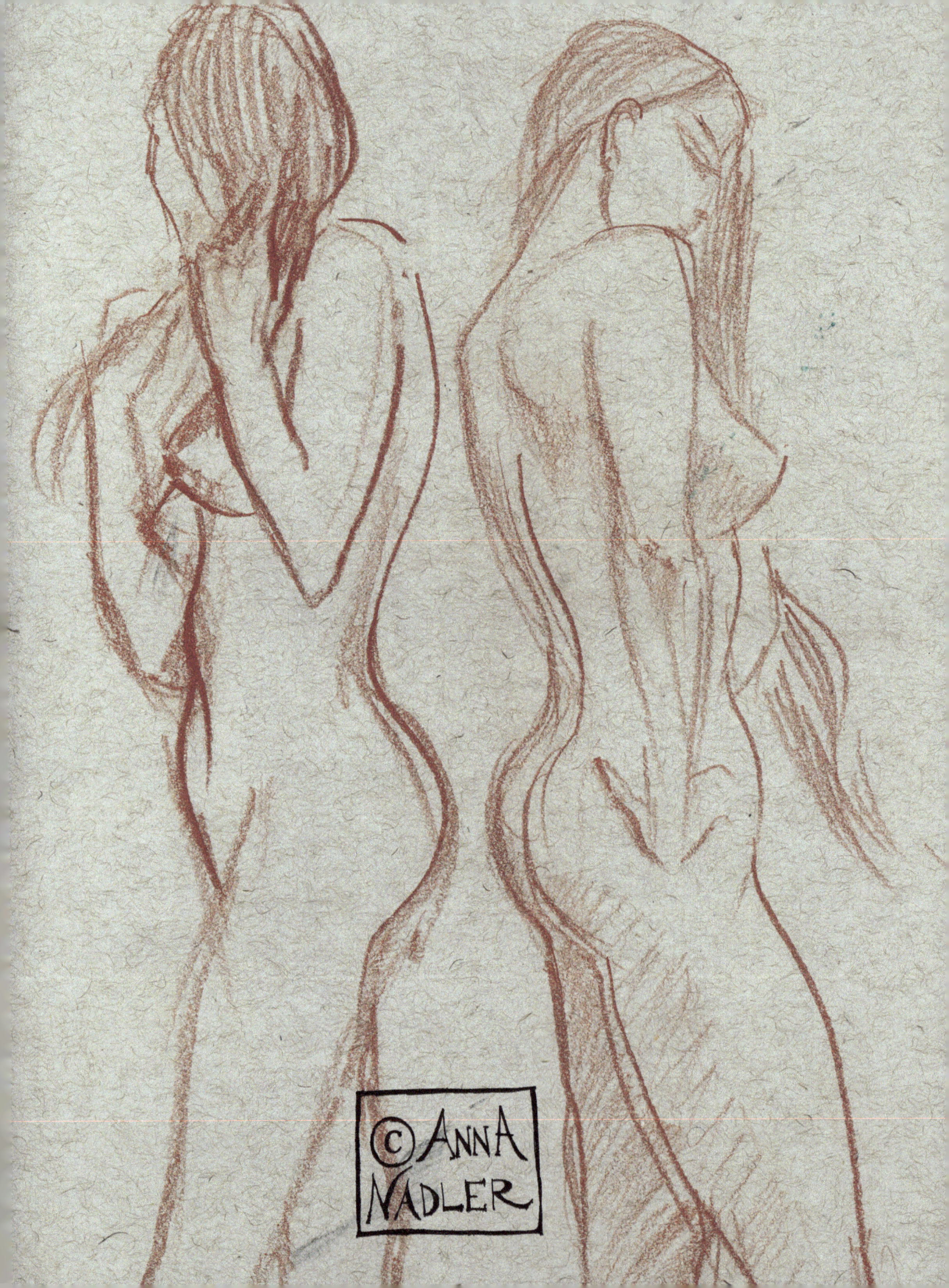

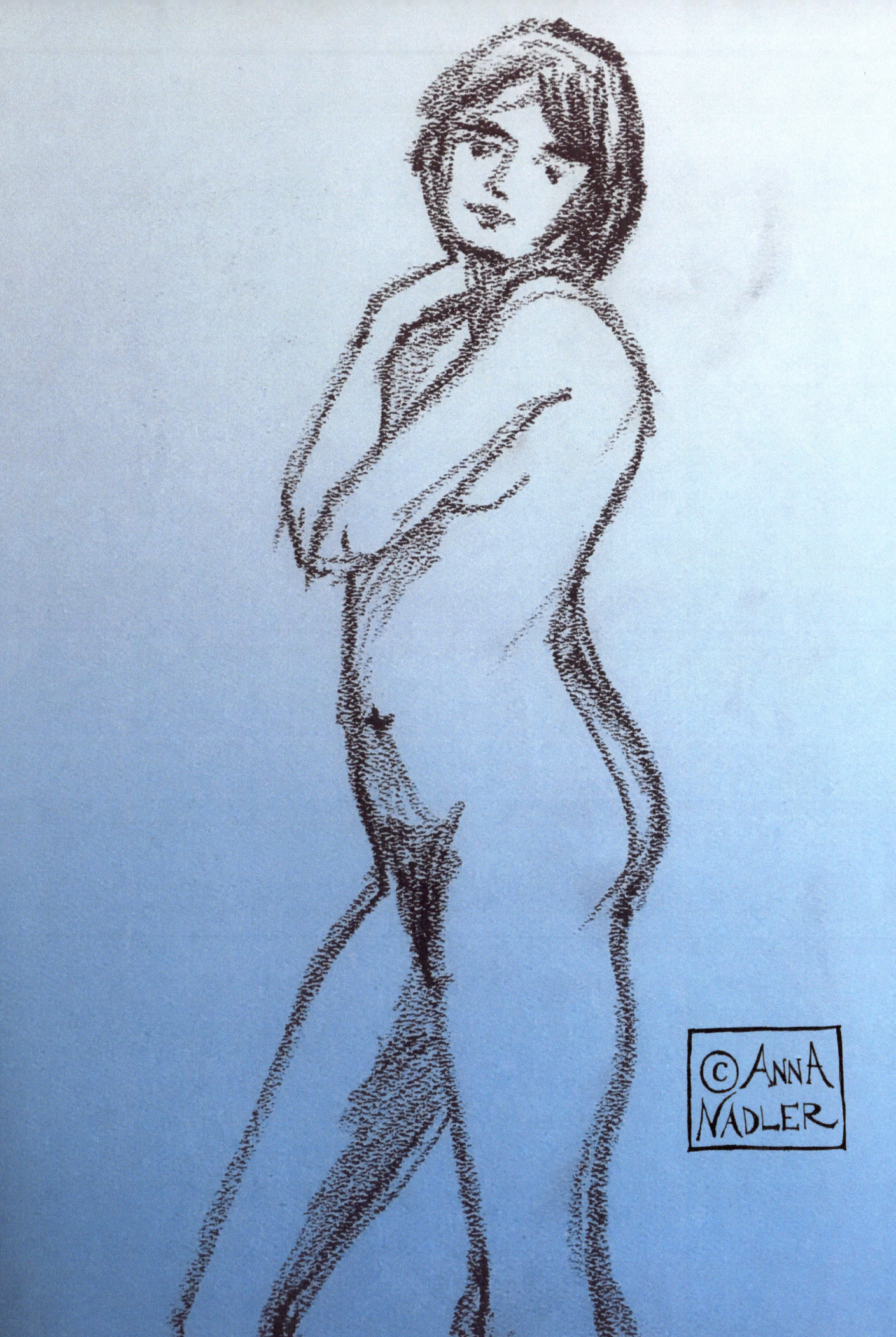

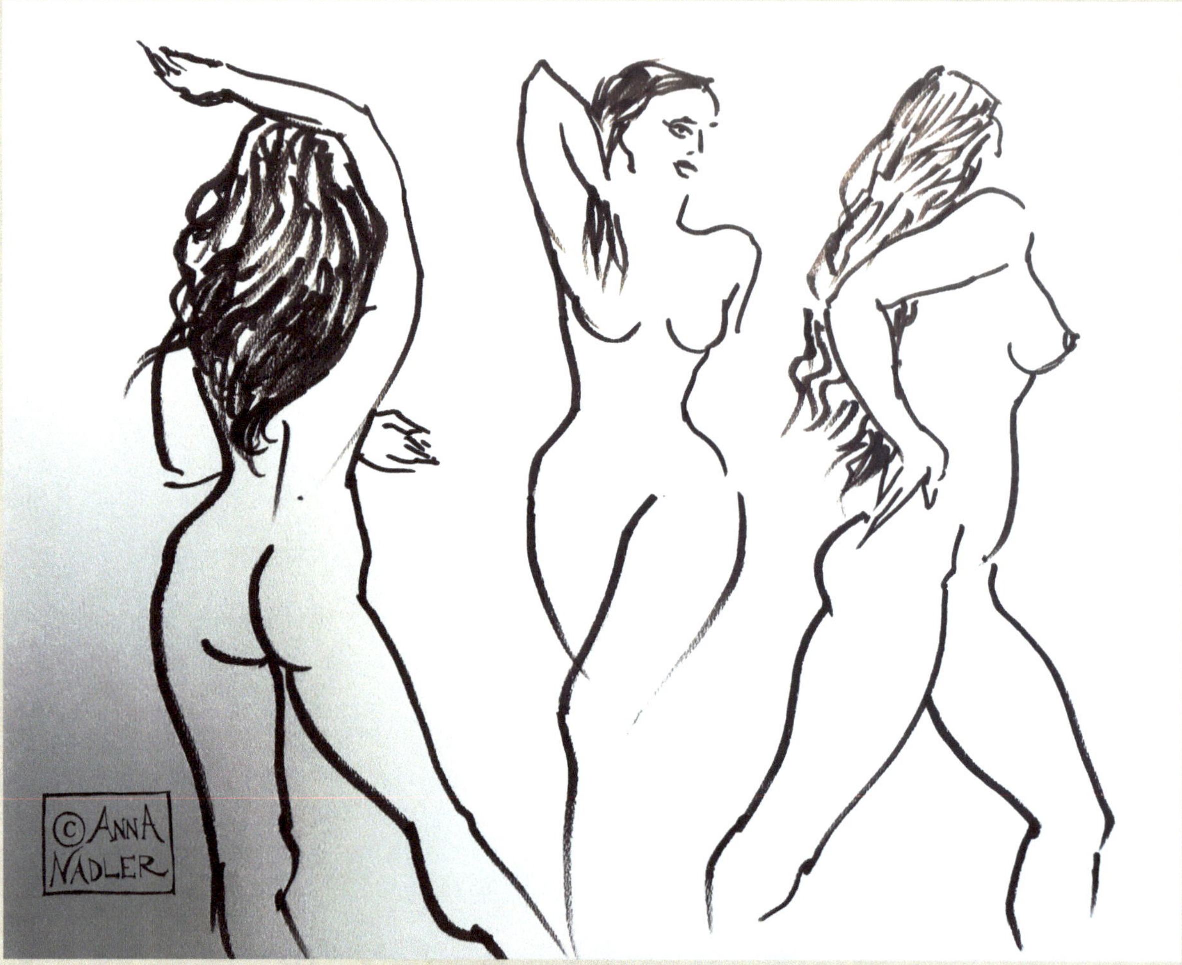

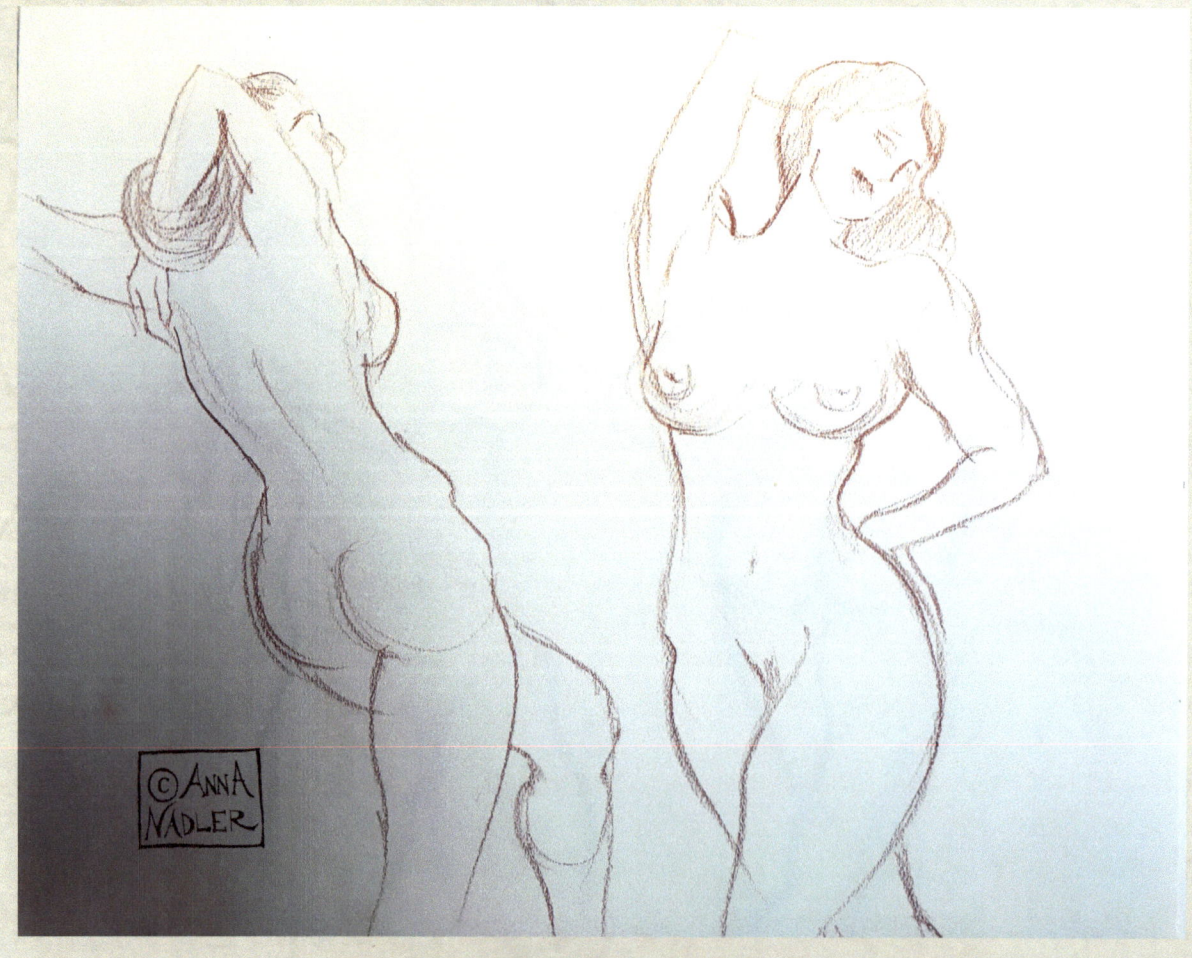

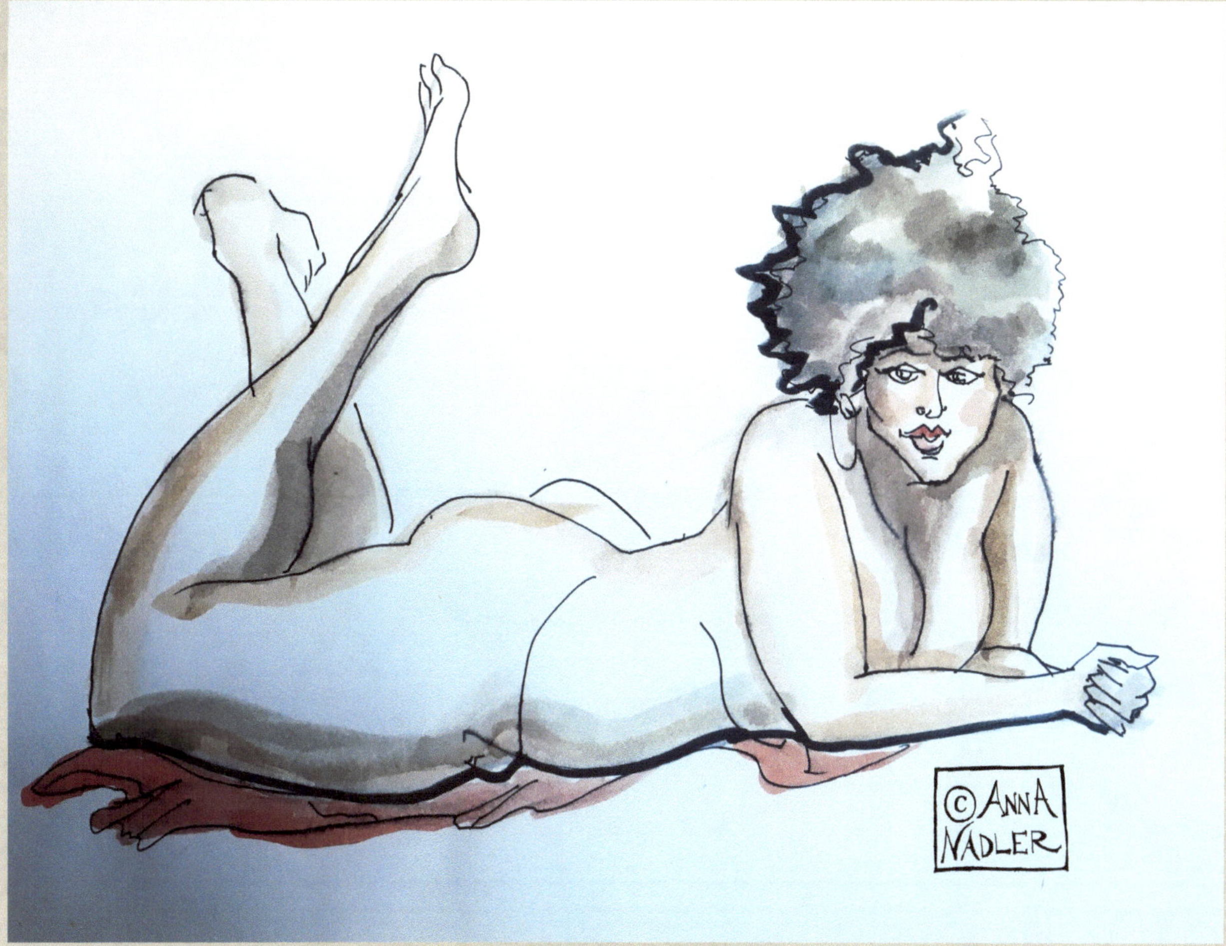

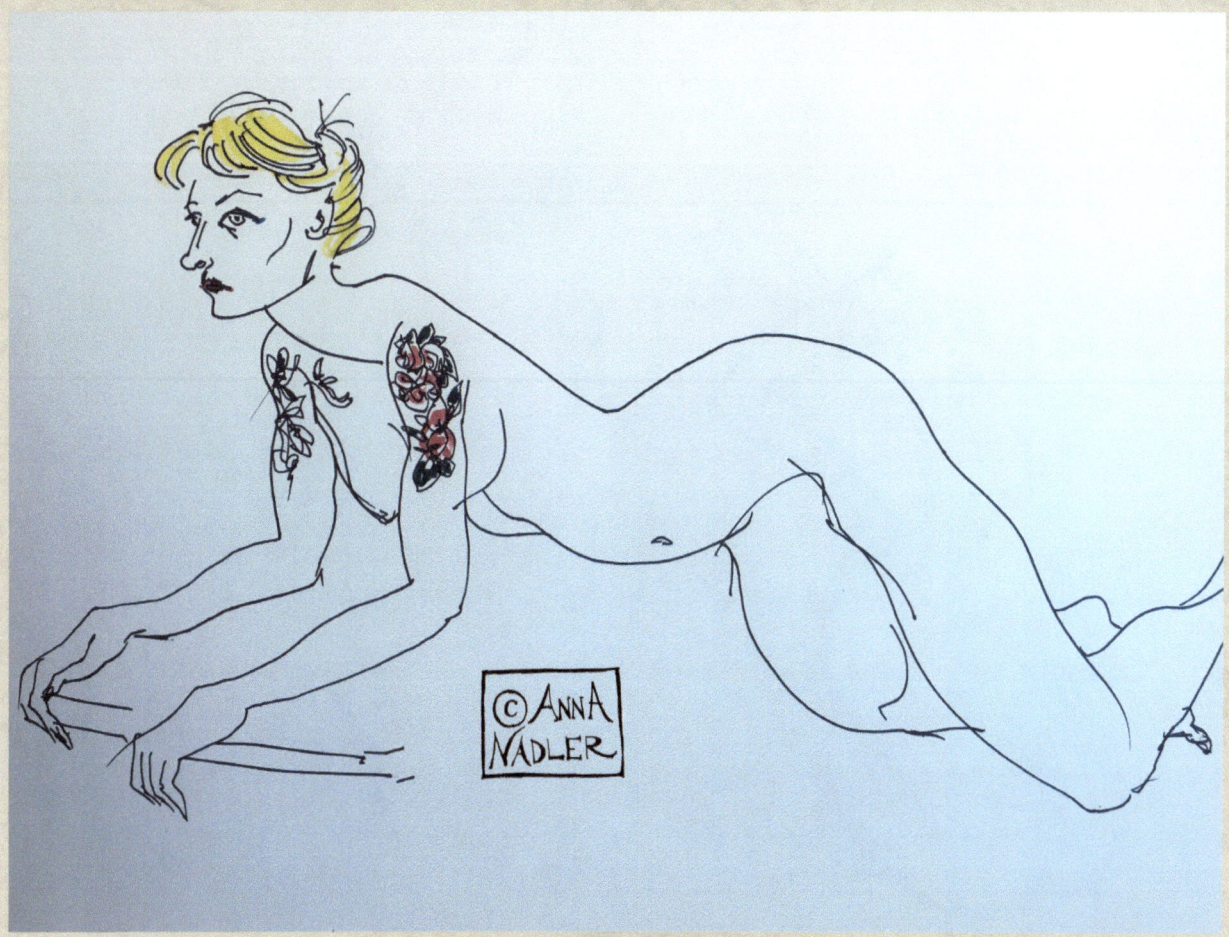

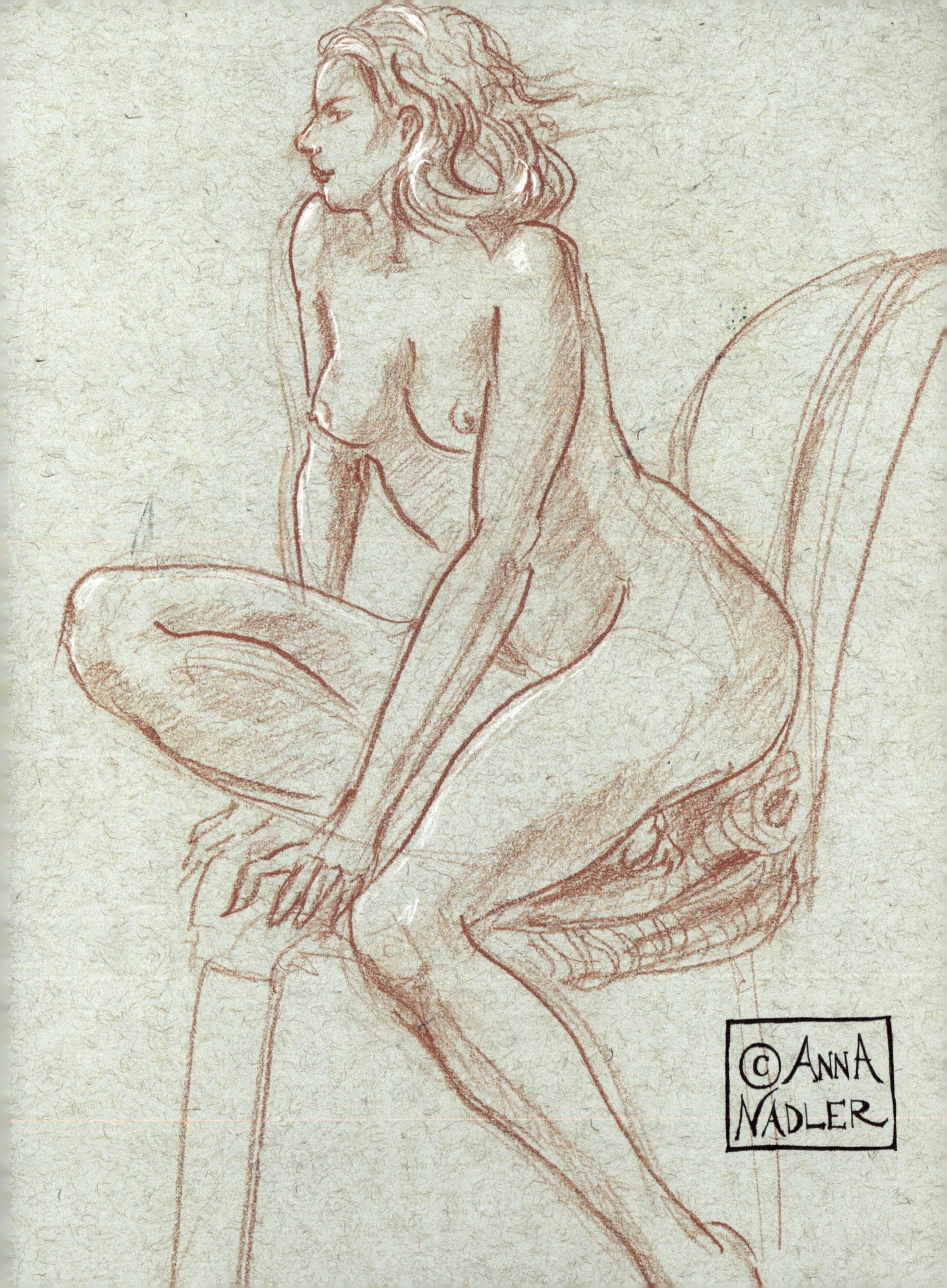

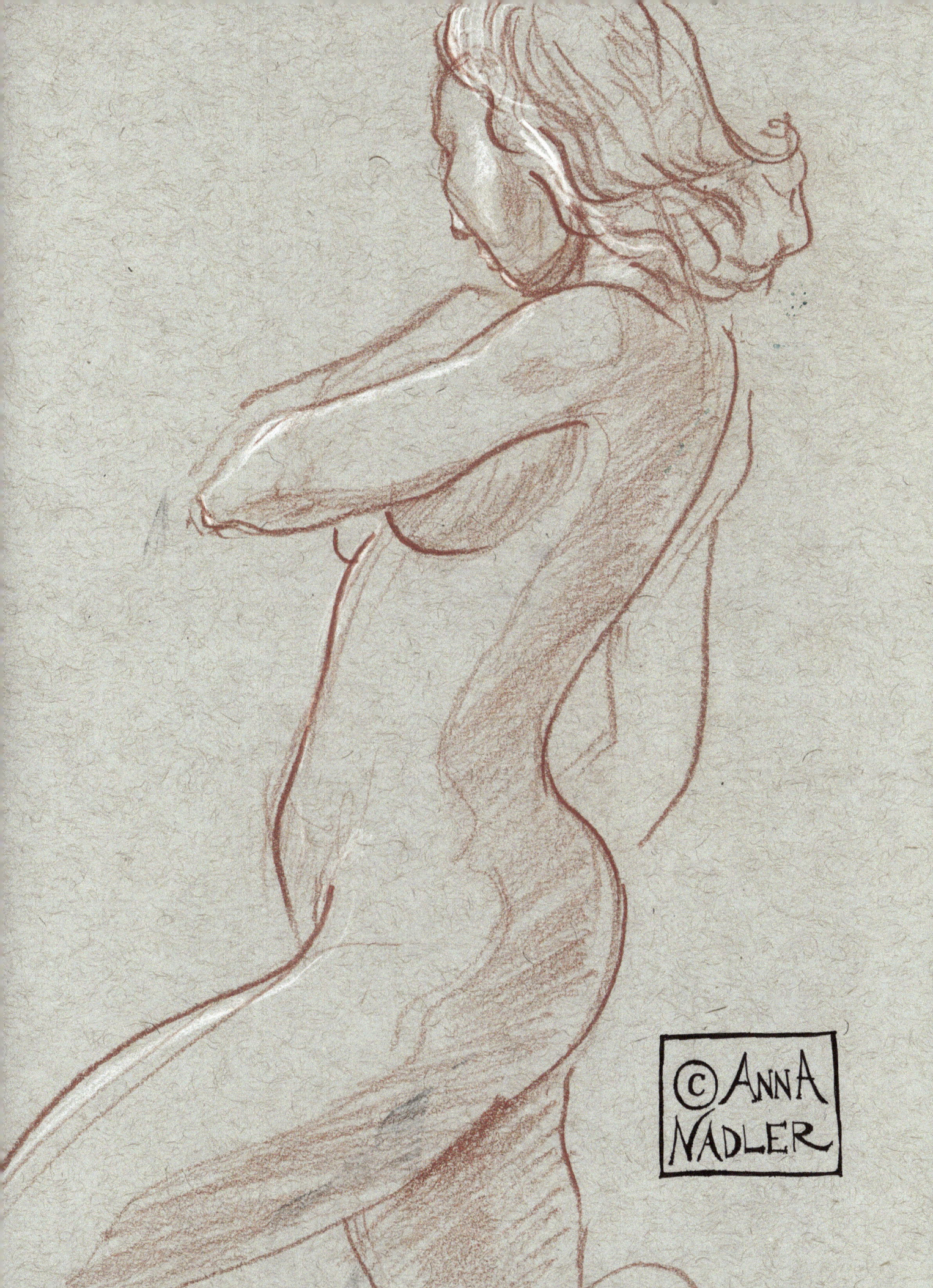

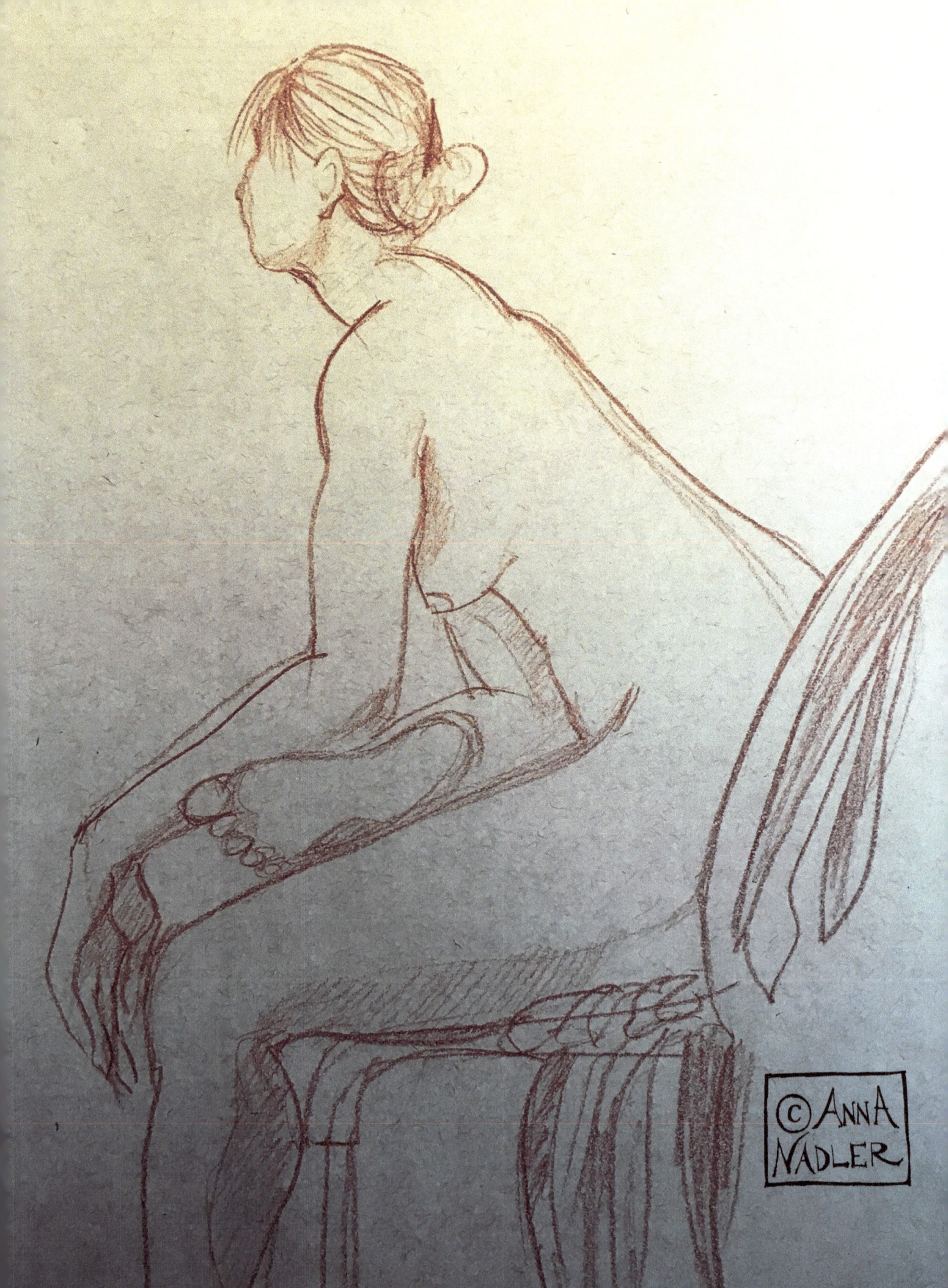

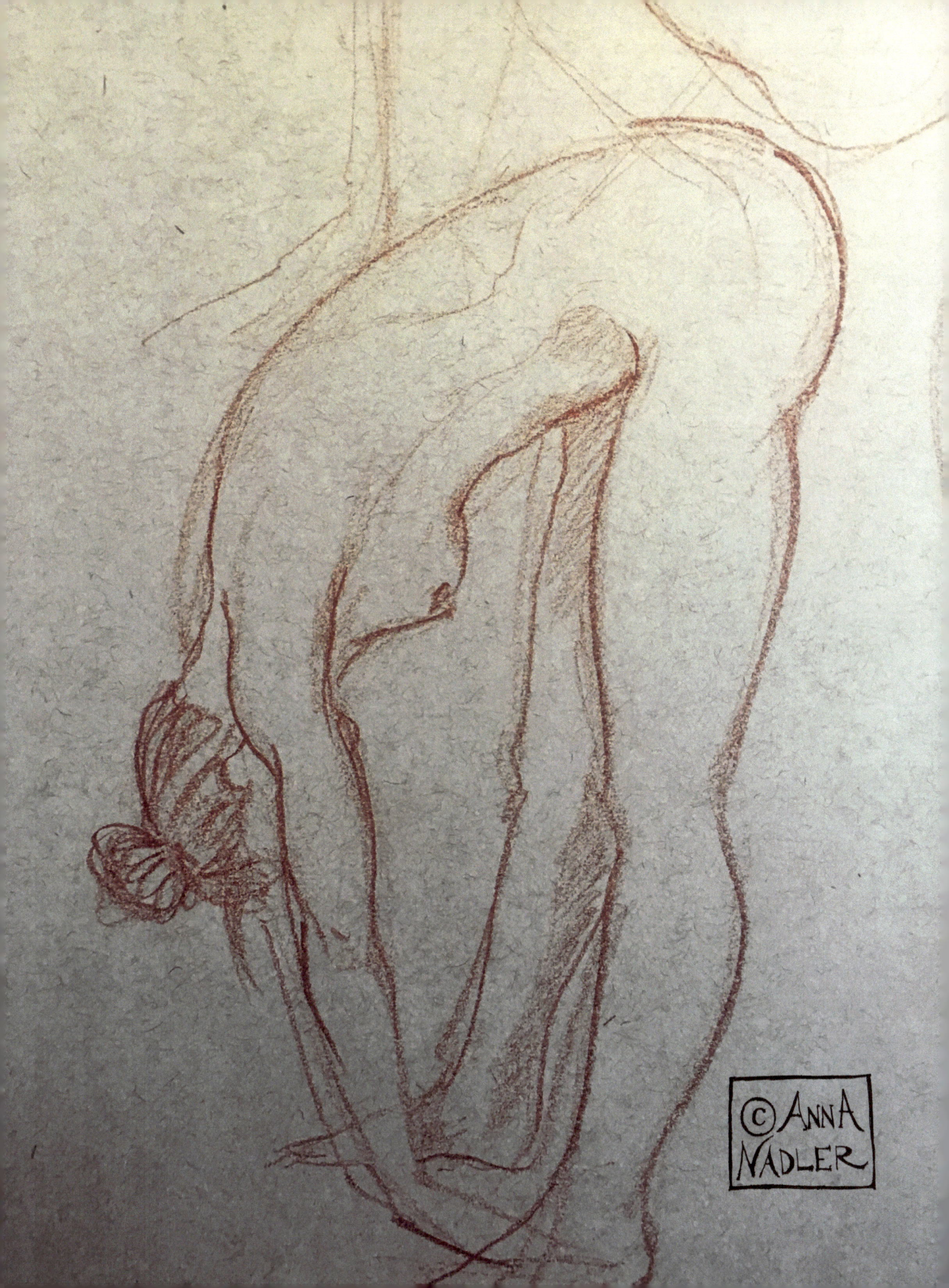

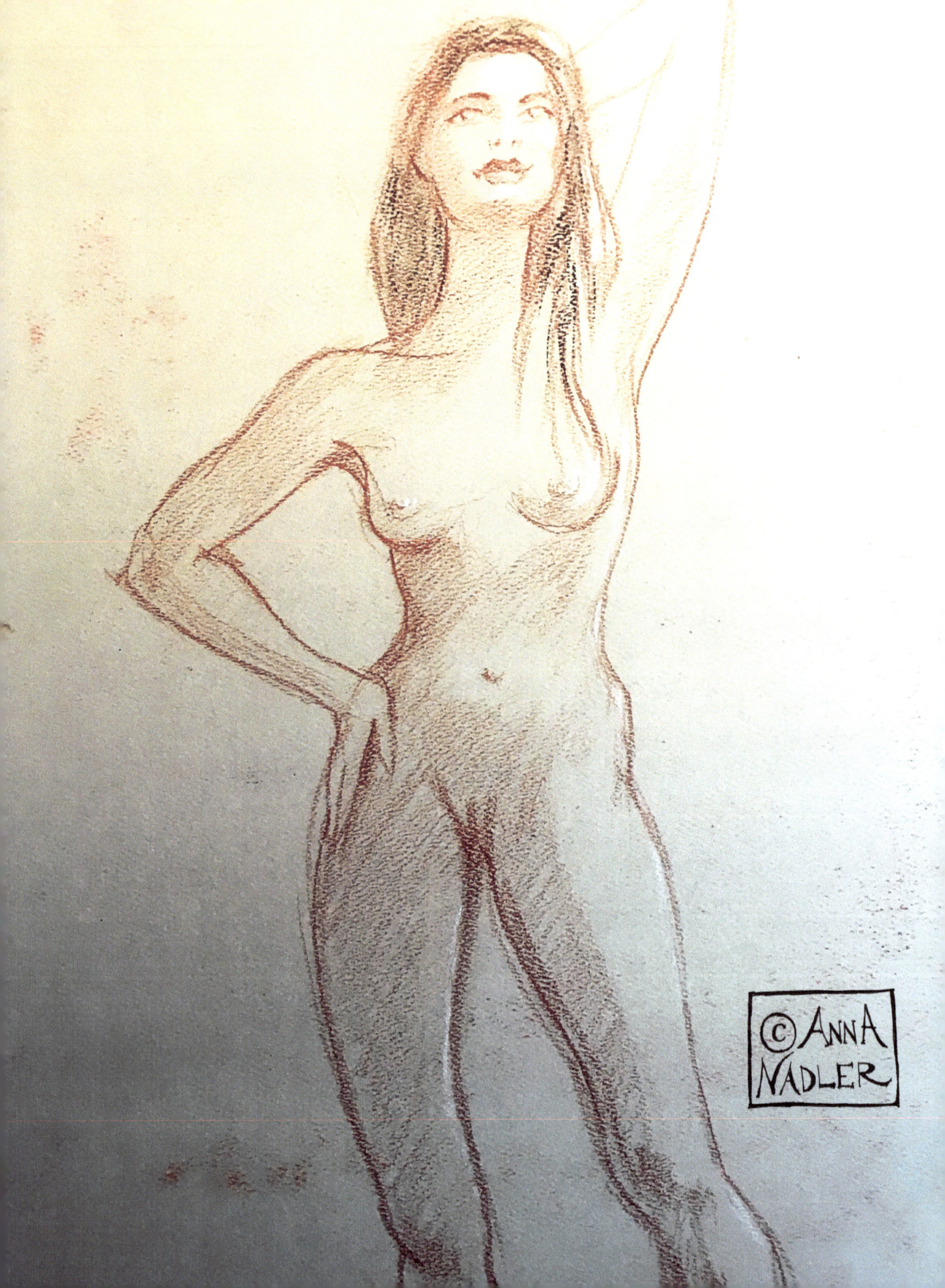

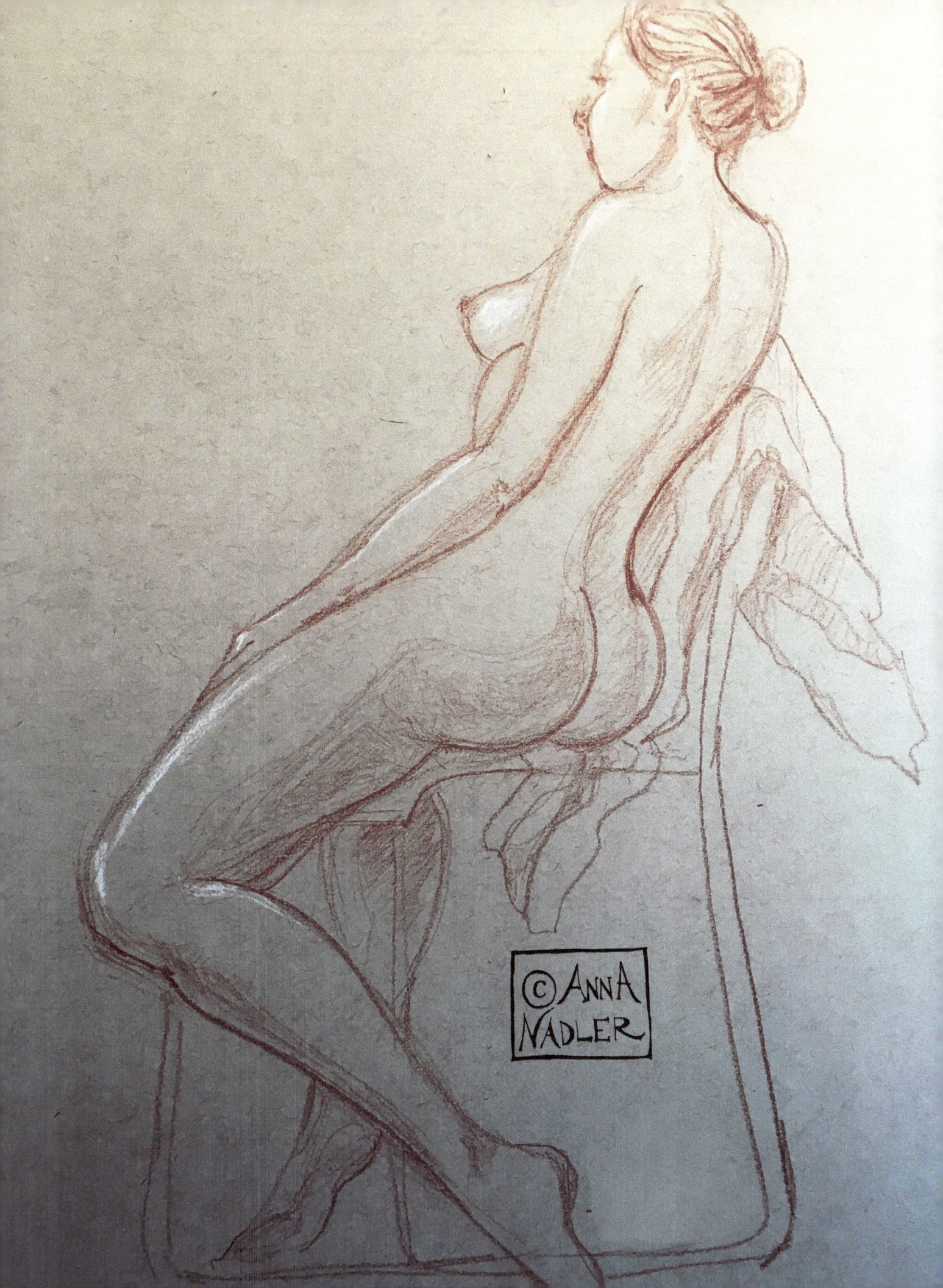

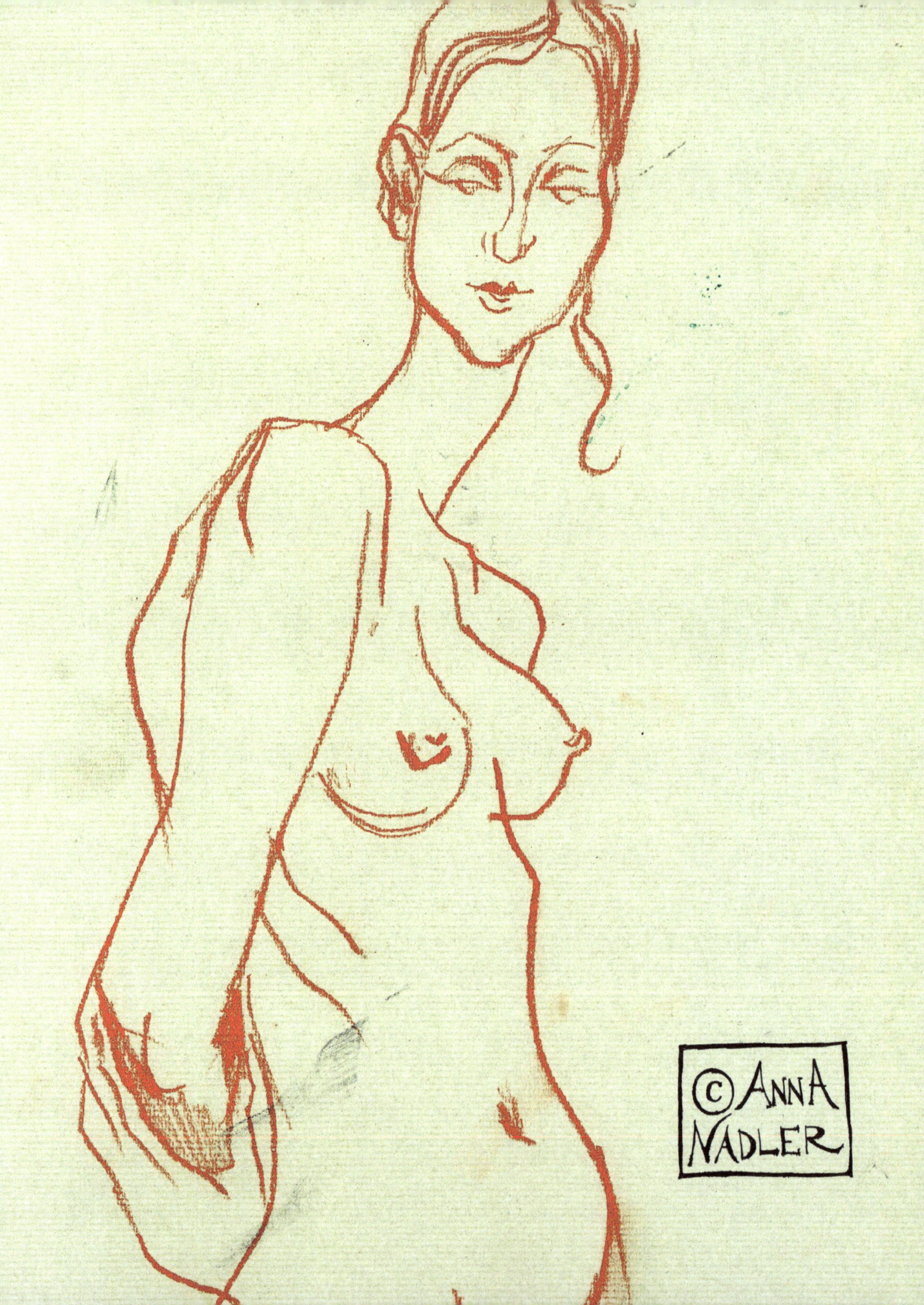

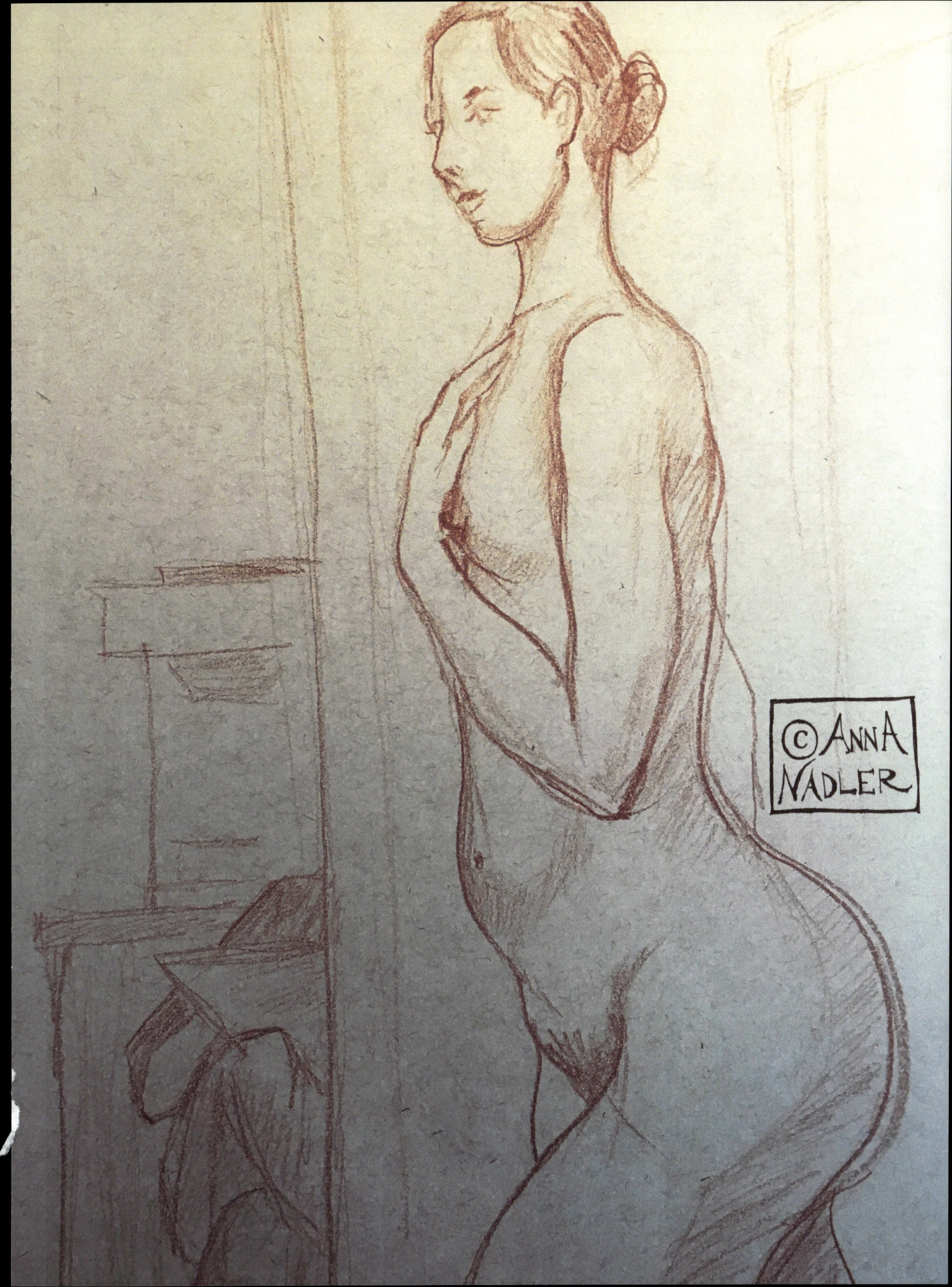

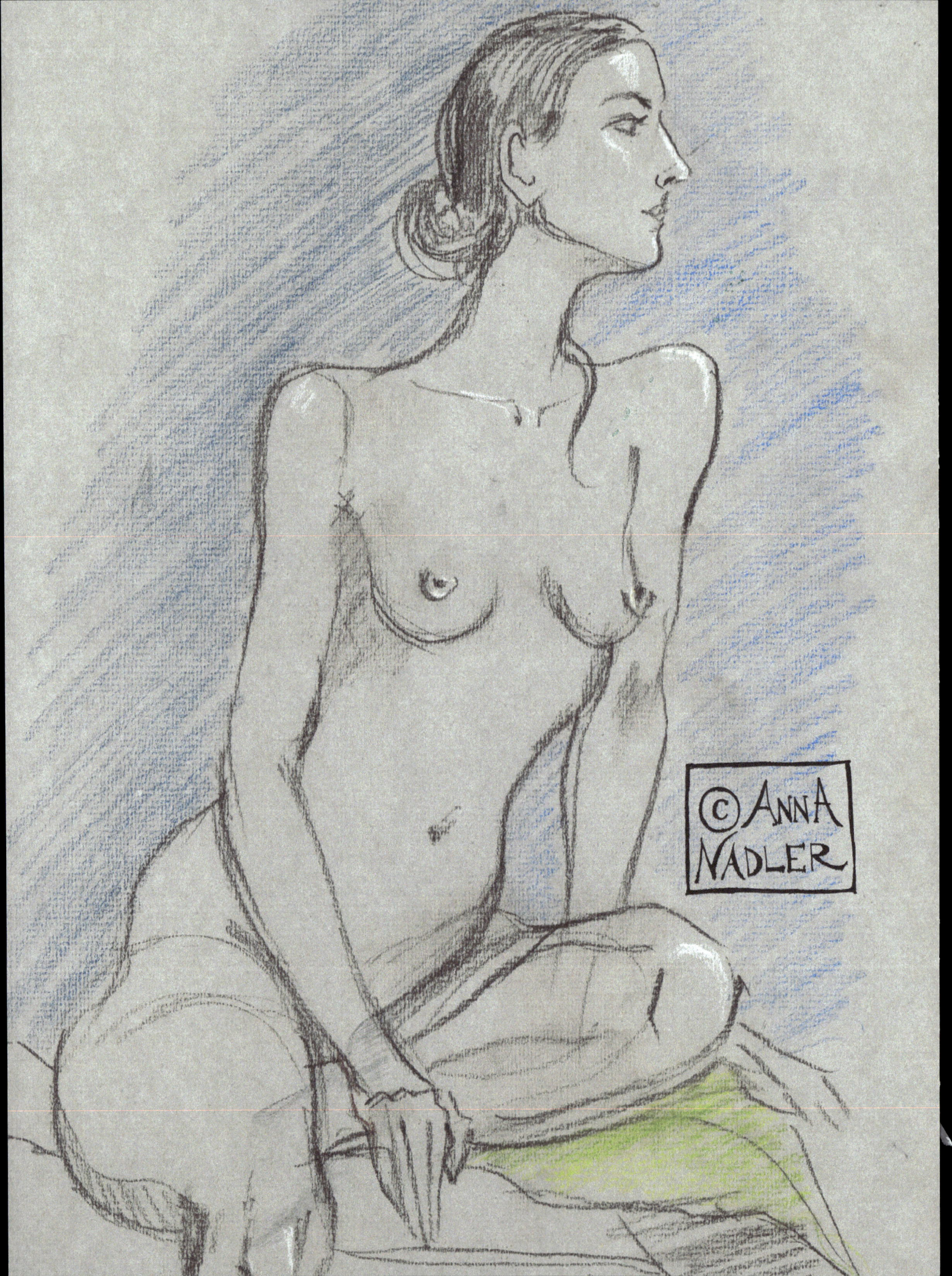

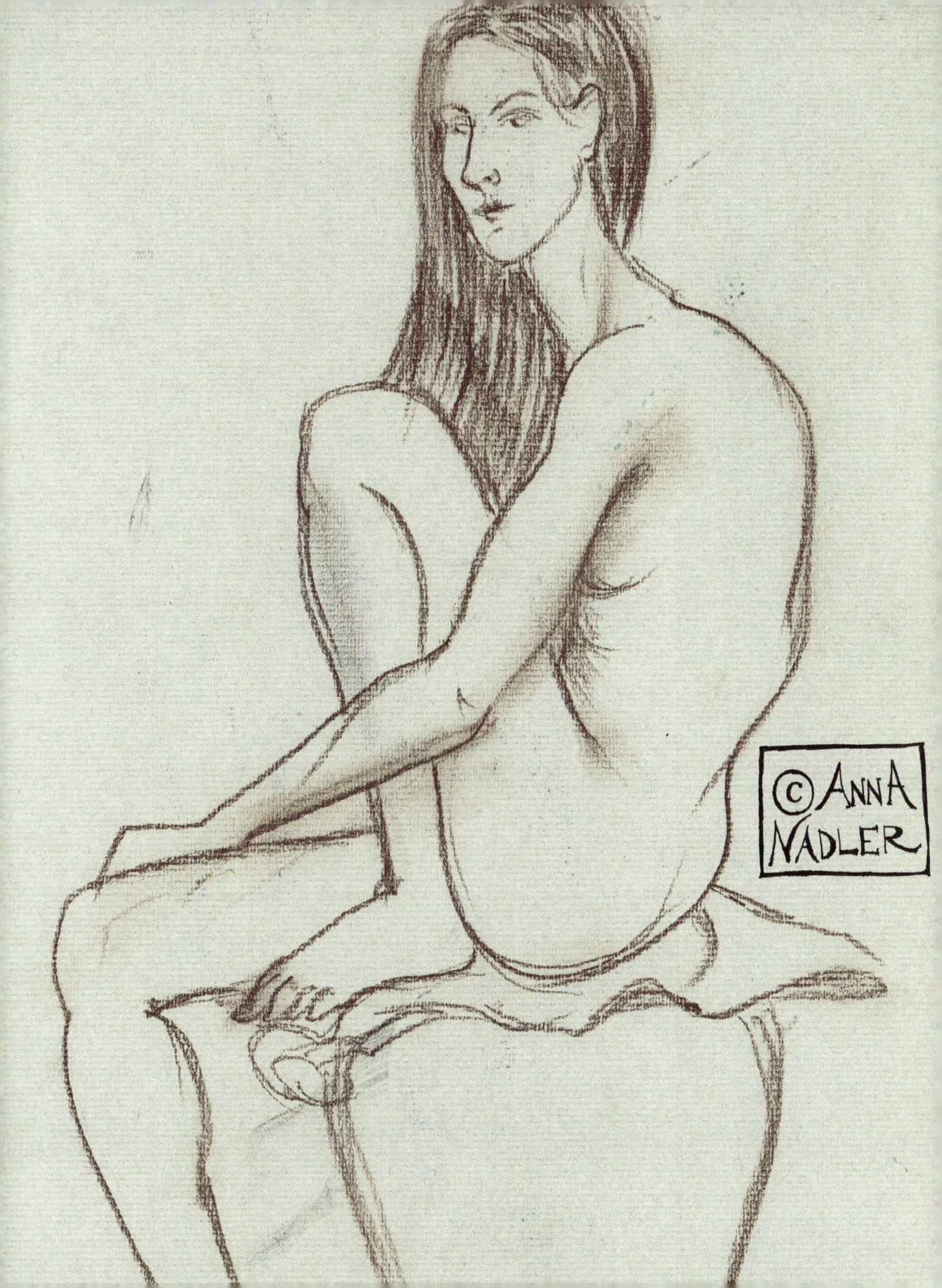

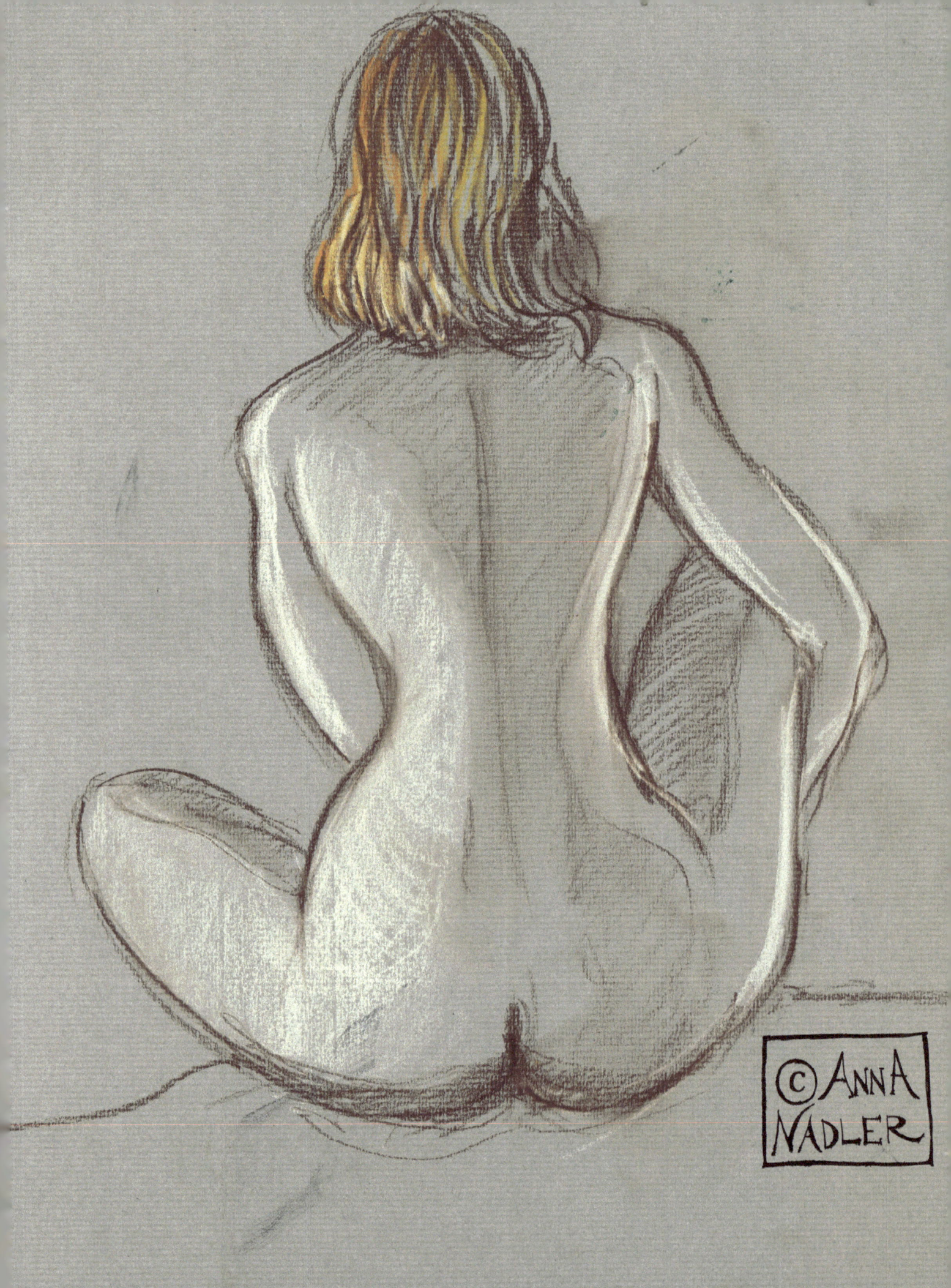

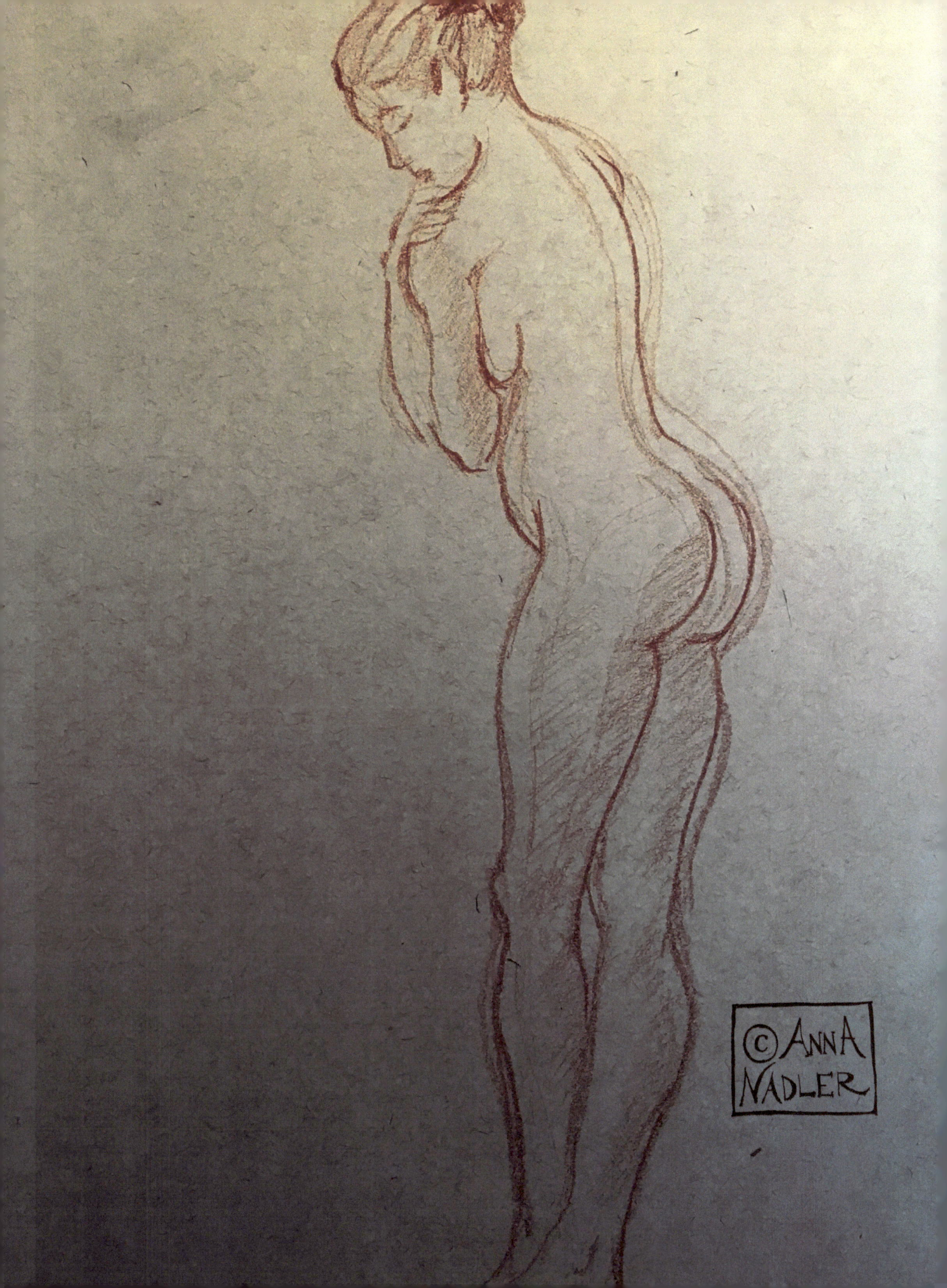

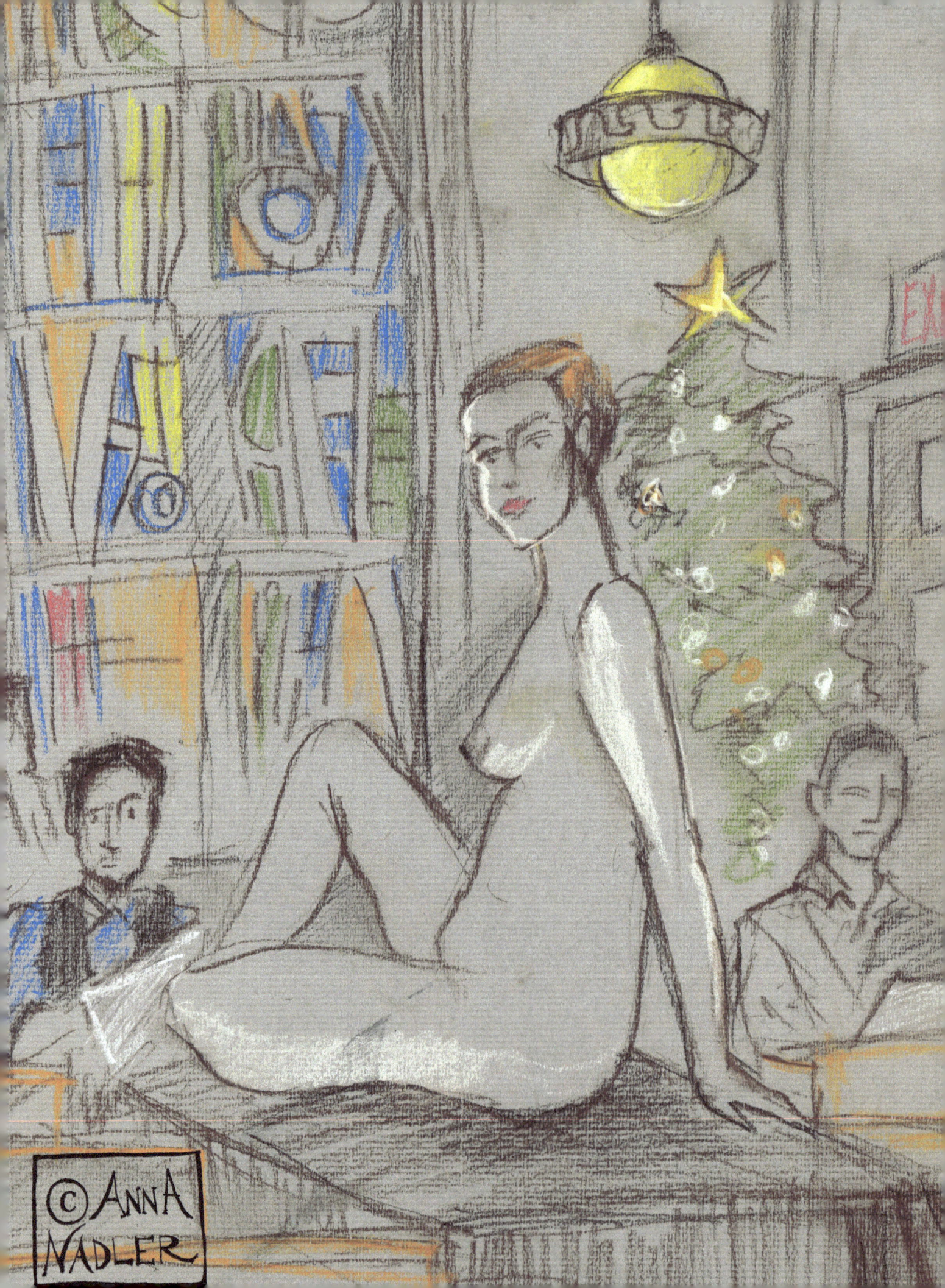

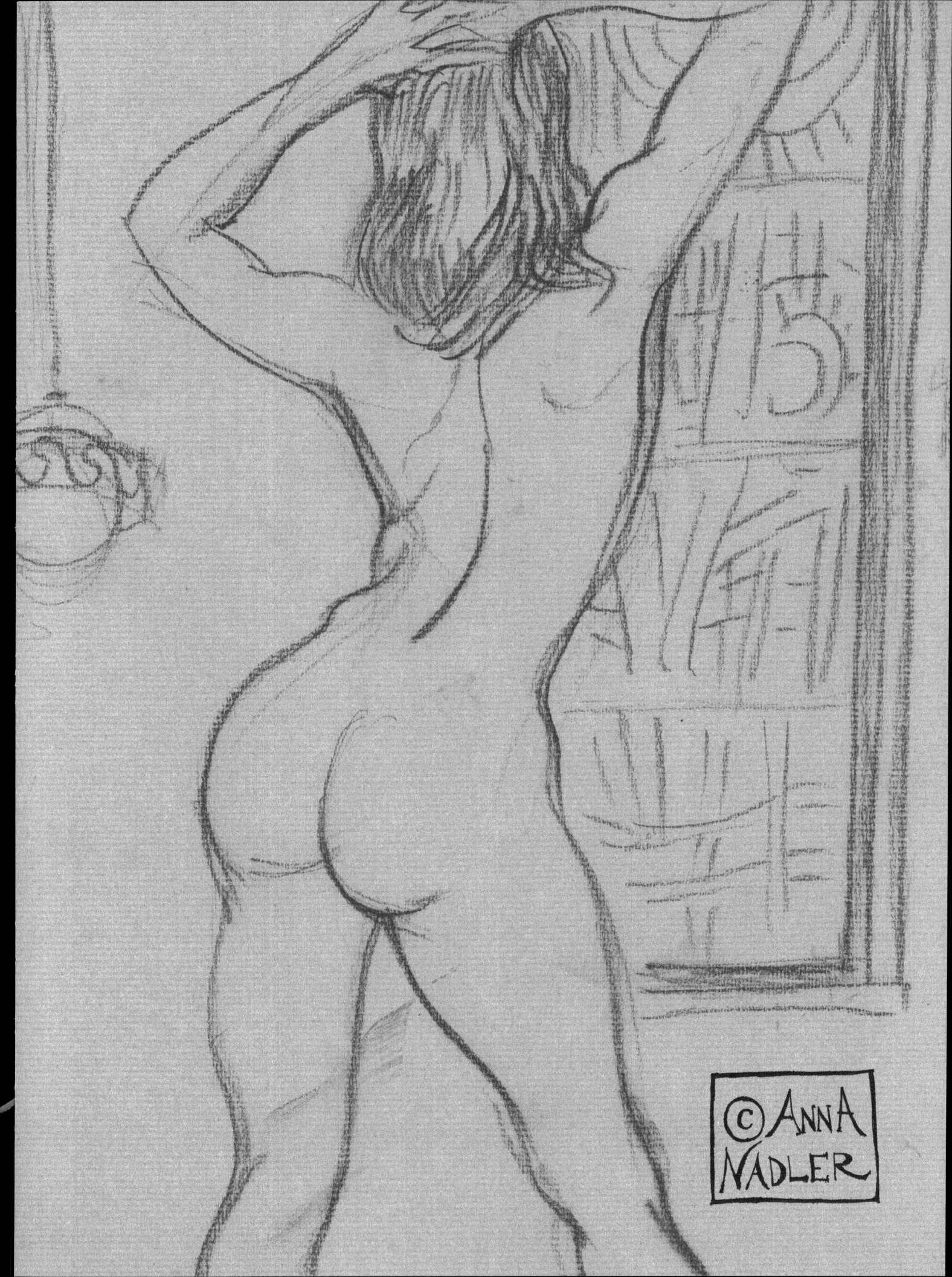

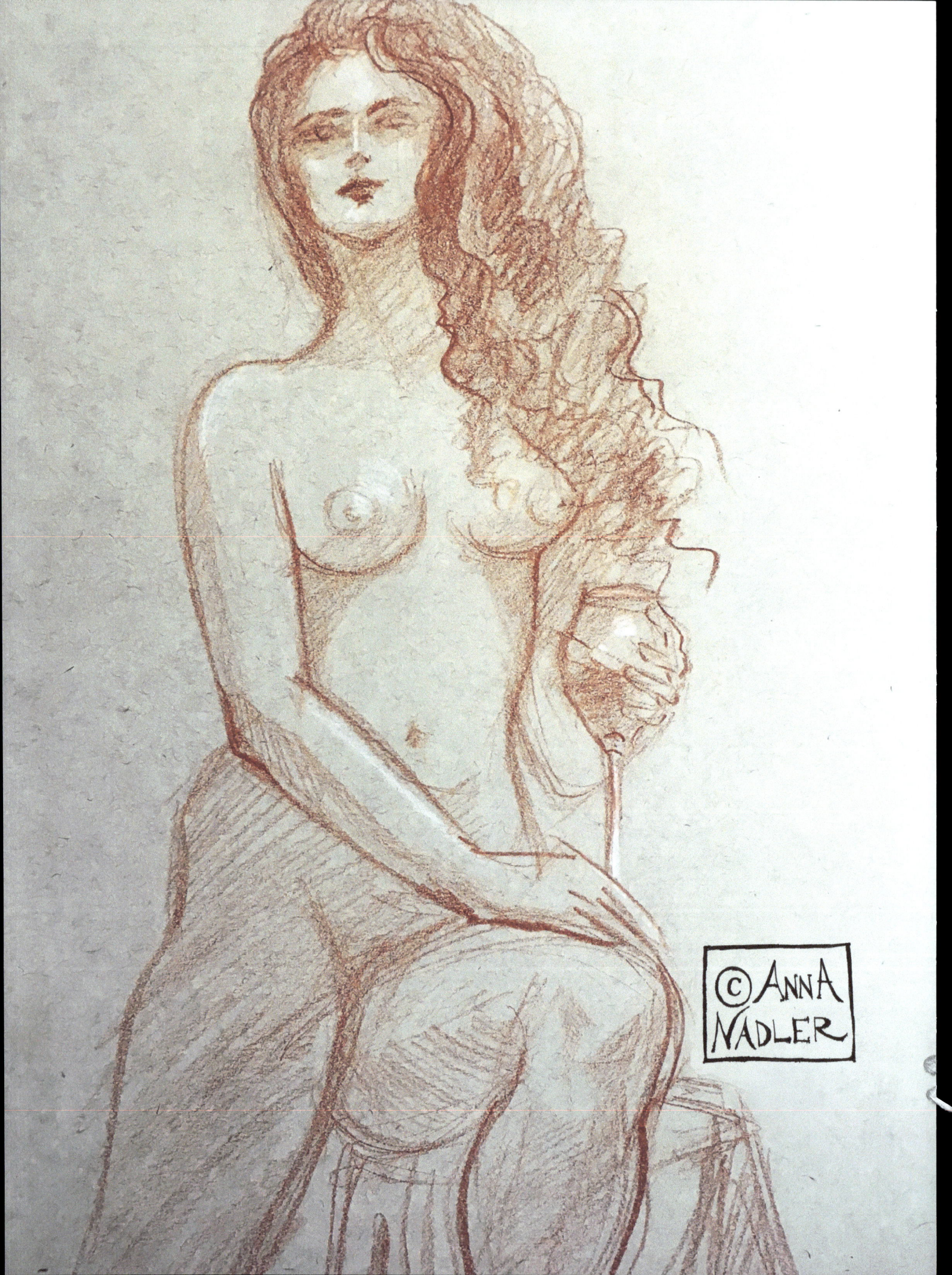

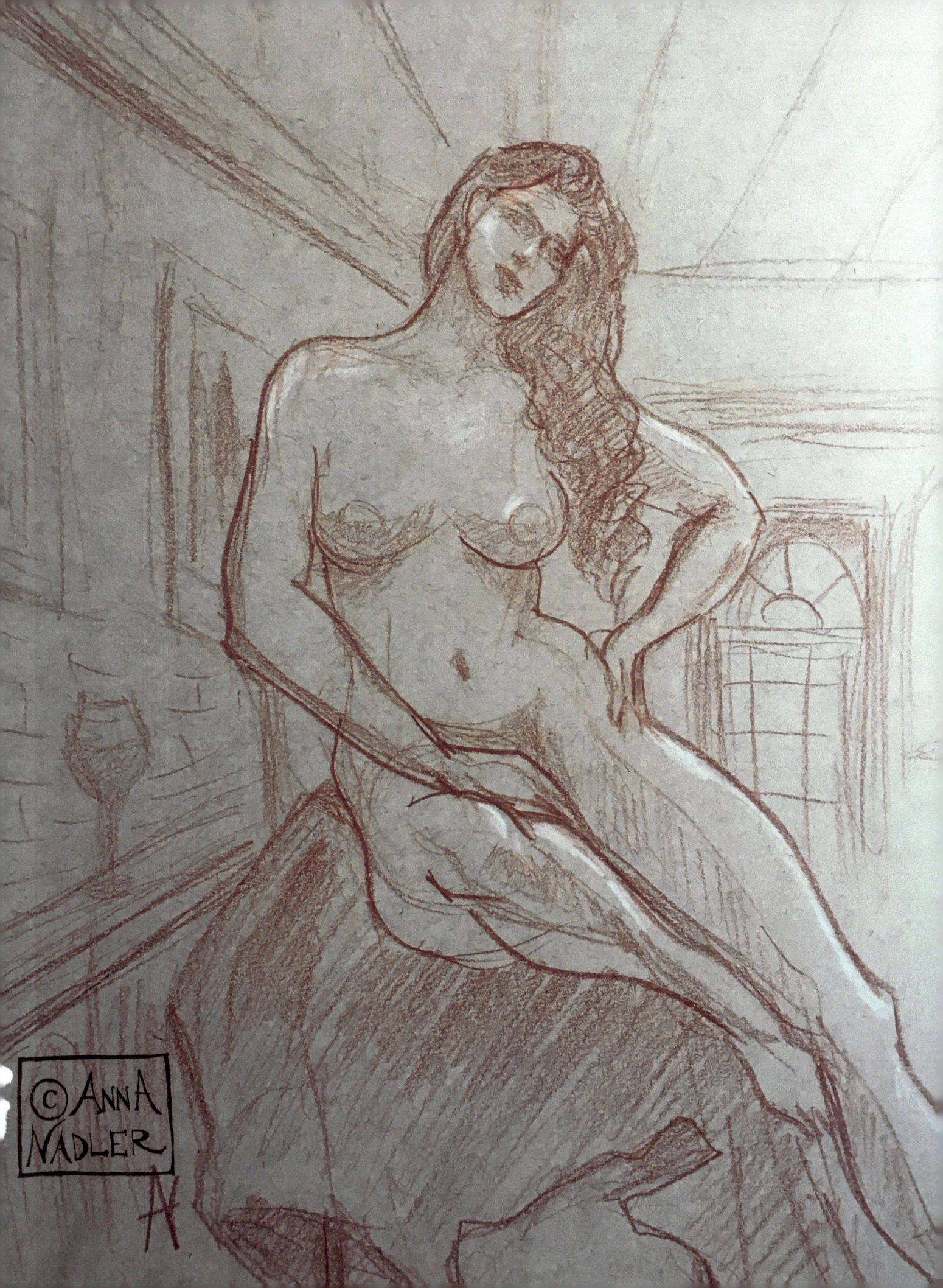

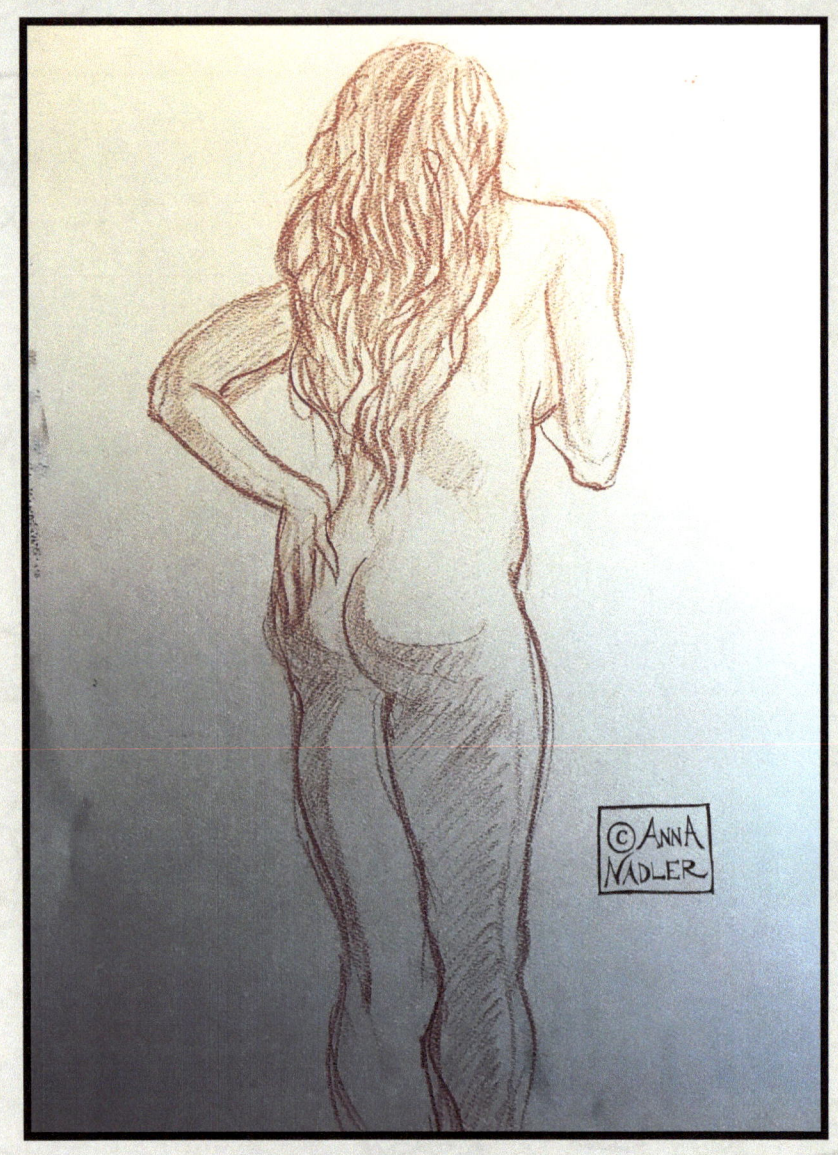

Thank you for viewing the collection of "Manhattan Nudes."
If you enjoyed this book, please feel free to leave a review on Amazon.com.

Thank you!

Anna

www.ingramcontent.com/pod-product-compliance
Lightning Source LLC
Chambersburg PA
CBHW051221220526
45473CB00003B/1122